FORGIVE, FORGET, AND RELEASE!

ANNA DANIEL

BALBOA.
PRESS

A DIVISION OF HAY HOUSE

Balboa Press books may be ordered through booksellers or by contacting:

Balboa Press
A Division of Hay House
1663 Liberty Drive
Bloomington, IN 47403
www.balboapress.com.au
1 (877) 407-4847

Print information available on the last page.

ISBN: 978-1-5043-0841-0 (sc)
ISBN: 978-1-5043-0840-3 (e)

Balboa Press rev. date: 06/07/2017

INTRODUCTION

This book has been written to help guide and light the way for the many searching souls. It has been a great help to myself and so I hope it will be to many other genuine souls that are looking for a connection and a way to understand what life is all about. The Universe has been my main teacher from within my big team and therefor is credited for each reading – TttA, (The truth through Anna)

I also wish to thank Bruce for his assistance with editing and grammar and endless hours of typing and composition of the book and proof reading and support. Also a big thank you to all teachers, masters and healers that have aided me in order to complete this book. You can also use the book, opened at random to get a message from the source.

The pace and chaos that often surrounds today's world has prompted many of us to search for answers to life's greatest questions. In an enlightening, spiritually uplifting guidebook, medium Anna Daniel connects with the other side to provide guidance to searching souls seeking inner-peace, an understanding of the meaning of life, and the motivation to move forward on their spiritual journeys.

Within easily digestible paragraphs, Anna provides clear direction from good spirits anxious to influence and instruct others on daily living. She leads others down an empowering path that encourage a focus on living one day at a time, remaining true to ourselves and our dreams, embracing challenges as opportunities to grow, trusting in our intuitions, finding gratitude, spreading kindness, and balancing our energy and lives overall.

Forgive, Forget, and Release! shares wisdom derived from spirit connections to guide and light the way for searching souls interested in living meaningful existences on Earth.

Love and light to all readers – from The Source

ANOTHER STEP UP ON THE LADDER!

Progress is being made so keep up the good work. When you look back you can easy see what was happening further back. Only by stepping up or aside you will get a clearer view and more insight. Things are unfolding and not the way or time that you thought, but all is working in your time. You know that is divine timing and the very best for you at your pace. Today one more task will be accomplished. That is what we mean a day at a time. Rather a task at a time. You got extra support and help last night. And we did hear your prayers. A fresh start in many areas will benefit many and your work will increase again. You are getting more insight and very strong. Let us keeping on teaching, healing and guiding all of your past away from many others so called knowledge. Many egos get in the way and make beliefs too naïve and lacking in judgement as to who is who. It's all a part of development so look at it with compassion, love and light. Carry out what is for today and give thanks to the universe.

Amen to that. TttA

FOCUS ON ENERGY OUTPUT!

Let the New Year begin in a healthy way and keep a sharp eye on where your energy goes. It's when you see where the energy goes. It's very beneficial when you see the signs and recognise the symbols of good energy. You therefore can aid your work and let us give you the channels that would be beneficial for you. This year is another part of your journey. It's been an unusual and in more than one way and you still have a lot of odd things happening but that's a part of your life's learning. Many new chapters of enlightenment are coming to you. You have now to open up to be able to connect faster and hear us better. Still we understand you more than many others. Most see only a part of you and it is the part that will help them. Most can feel a glimpse from us so they want more by following through with our teachings. Like a strong current of water can drag you down and a roaring force can lift you up. The river of life is like that. There are many variations of events to test and explain to you all.

Love and light TttA

ORDER!

Keep in mind, change around and shift place now and then. It will freshen up the feeling of renewal. In still days you can use the time to relax refresh and renew. Look at your environment inside and out. Think about colours and shapes. Would it benefit to alter? Let us give you the ideas that is best for you. It's individual how people react to alterations. Try out something new or alter your routine a little. Many get so used to certain pattern so it gets taken for granted. Instinct is also beneficial. Train yourself to just know how when and where what next is on the agenda. Look at nature and your pets. They follow instinct and what is wanted. We have told you all this for years now, so this is only a reminder. More work is coming in so get ready. Your overhaul is soon done. Recognition is to be looked at also, thankfulness and gratitude.

Eternal blessings. TttA

GROW AS YOU GO ON!

Everlasting learning is the key to life forever. Let's walk together beside each other. Others will go ahead or behind as extra help and support. Everybody will have a more distinct work order this year, specialised and very important. So many links in the chain all better qualified than last year. Keep on being better informed and stay with your particular part of work. Don't ever try to copy others or get away from your learning curve. That would not benefit anyone. There are no short cuts to higher growth. Steady doe's it, doing your routine work does not have to be drudgery. Think of it as a brick at a time, building your spirit fort for further use, for all mankind. It's a privilege to be able to serve the universal aim. Still we are reminding you that you all are energy output and input so use it wisely Keep in mind to do only your part and leave the rest to us.

Joyful blessings and peace. TttA

KEEP UP YOUR DISCIPLINE!

Some days it will seem too much and other days it will come naturally. It's a part of life and how to understand which way to deal with it. Ask and you will receive ask in the name of the creator be very careful about the source and try to be one step ahead. Always do all your homework. And be honest about it. It's hard to know at times when and how. Go to your safe place and empty out and be ready to receive. You are getting plenty of practice every day so keep up the good work. Time will soon go and you need to remember to take time out. The silent time will recharge you and also outside is a good way to get energy. Today you have seen more, once again so much change in the energy levels of people and pets. Stay with us and we will look after you as we always have. Blessings are always sent your way whatever the situation.

Be still and know that I am God. Forever yours TttA

ORDER!

Keep in mind to do just that. Change around and shift place now and then it will freshen up the feeling of renewal. In still days you can use the time to relax refresh and renew. Look at your environment inside and out. Think about colours and shapes. Would it benefit to alter? Let us give you the ideas that are best for you. It's individual how people react to alterations. Try out something new or alter your routine a little. Many get so used to certain pattern so it gets taken for granted. Instinct is also beneficial. Train yourself to just know how when and where what next on the agenda. Lock at nature and your pets. They follow instinct and what is wanted. We have told you all this for years now, so this is only a reminder. More work is coming in so get ready. Your overhaul is soon done. Recognition is to be looked at also, thankfulness and gratitude.

Eternal blessings. TttA

CALM AND JOY IN THE STORM!

Show others the way as we have shown you. The path is stormy at times, but that's so you can learn and be vigilant. To smooth the way will make you take things for granted and you would not be listen the same. Life needs to flow and when blockages appear that makes you think and ask questions. It's quite O K to ask aloud but to ask too much at once is not good. Focus on one area at the time otherwise it will easy get tangled up or get confused. Whatever your talent is we know exactly and we will give you the answers in your language. Easy for your understanding and level of growth. We are not giving too many answers at once as you could not deal with it in an acceptable way. If we don't reach anyone it's because of us the person needs to empty out and get ready for more input. It's quite a natural process and you have to think about the store house being full and ready to be used. As the level goes down you need to refill. Don't leave it to the last minute to get a refill or as you say top ups.

Eternal blessings to all. TttA

ETERNAL LOVE!

The word love is not often use on your planet in its original meaning. To fully understand its use you need to look at what eternal and universal have done and will do. Sit in silence and ask for an explanation in a way that you will understand. Because of your different levels of growth you would do best getting a specific picture. What's suitable to one would not necessarily be good for the other. The human spirit, mind, emotion and body is often more delicate than you know. Go easy on your fellow man, all is not in the picture that you first encountered. Wait for your answer until you are getting the O K. First connect with the person's spirit and you will know what to do next. This year is going to be an unfolding for many. Stand by and still do your living and studying. To grow is to advance and so it goes on. Let the fresh wind blow life in to your souls.

Blessings for your work. TttA

LET THE STORM CLEAR THE AIR AND THE RAIN WASH AWAY WHAT'S NOT NEEDED!

Well now, let the nature forces help and guide you in your quest. Everyone would do well at least sharing out to grow in this new blessed year. If you are already on your journey for spirit connections upwards and onwards will be your motto for this New Year. Remember to check and ask us. You all have talents and abilities so use them for healing helping and holiness. At times we give you three words starting with a letter to help you to understand our work for your book rather ours will be better received than the two first ones because many more are ready to read and listen. Let today make another brick in your progress and strength. Your spirit force must be strong, steady and secure. Let our love, light and life secure enhance your day and others .Enjoy little things and count your blessings.

Rich reward is yours. TttA

HOLD ON!

Please don't give up now when the part of the race is going to slow and where the goal is soon in sight .It's all done in stages because human DNA is not fully developed as yet. We fully understand why the feelings and physical expressions are more evident and present. You can't alter one area and not see a change in others. You of all people have seen a lot of that lately. You also have to learn to cooperate and coordinate more with us. Many are trying very hard and getting tired so they start to query many events. That is natural that you would like to see and hear more of the big picture. You will see wonders unfold and many miracles just as it was when I was still on Earth. Earth as you have seen it and studied for many years now is about to alter quite considerably. It's all a big undertaking so have patience and persistence and be prepared. You would not be able to bear all in one picture so we only give you a piece sat the time. Bless all living things.

Eternally yours. TttA

LET THE SOUND HEAL YOU!

To go with the flow and soak up all the healing livings sounds of nature, music and power. You will recharge fast faster when you start your day in a connected way. To the areas. Walk amongst your garden and listen in to what Mother Nature brings. Peace and tranquillity will enter. Your soul to fill it for the whole day .That is what we meant when we talk about spirit food .The most important part of your feeding and nurturing. Make sure you full up your quota each day .The rest of your body mind and emotion will also benefit. First must be the first always. Spirit must be in charge. Many today have started to wonder about deeper meanings and why. That's a healthy sign. Awaken and enjoy the day as it comes. It gives you another chance to rectify yours or somebody else's life. You don't always know what's going on so wait to its all clear. We will give you the details. Grow, help and smile for today. You soon will know what's on your path.

Joy laughter and security. TttA

STRONG IN THE UPHEAVALS

Make sure that you follow through when we suggest changes or ask you to wait a while. The timing at present is so important and little too soon would not work, as we as you have waited. Back to divine timing. And ask us what the pattern and purpose with your quest. You also would miss out on an important connection that you got proof of the other day. You know that very well there is such thing as coincidences. It's a map that is individual for each person and development. As we have pointed out so many times before. It's a travel throughout time and space. You all are here to learn clean or connect with others from so many life times. Past what's needed is to sort out and give, and back so your slate can be clean and wipe out and get ready. Past mistakes and misguidance have to be deleted. Go out in my name and claim for change.

Blessed be with love and light through your everlasting team. TttA

ENJOY LIFE!

Find something to enjoy so you can so you can help your whole system to heal and help others. It might be only little happenings but all the same it could trigger of bigger events. The whole thing is to keep on going never to stay in the same groove. Still pause a while and give your spirit a chance to catch up. Beware of staying too long in the same stop. It would easy hinder you looking at other ideas or news. Refreshment and rest is natural and you just know when to do it. It's good to be in tune with yourself and nature. Use the nature forces to your advantage and still send love and light in return. An exchange is always the best way. Also remember the timing if not the condition is right it will not appear. Be patient and compassionate and know when to let go and we take over. Keep the good memories and let go of experiences that did you anything good. Only make you sad to see what people do to themselves and to others. Keep in mind what we have said and use it next time you have disturbance.

We know that you know. TttA

STEADY AS SHE GOES!

Carry on as you are, smile, heal and grow. All life is everlasting and the spirit is the life. So you can now explain better why, what and when. You all know what's going on when you connect with the source and the living god, the power of all creation and life force. You are getting more alert and not so easy affected of outside forces. Give all the last months thoughts of thankfulness and grace. Give also thanks for help given in one way or the other. Carry out your tasks today in the best way as possible. If you don't get the Ok wait. That principle stays whatever the circumstances. Things are unfolding and so wait a little longer. Divine timing is always present with you and for your work and strength. Your whole team is activated to guard all situations. New start with a part of your work and better communication line is prepared. Leave all your thoughts, cares and planes to us as we will give you input as you need it.

Loving warm feelings. TttA

VIGILANCE!

Guard yourself from side trackers. Many would try to get you involved in many subjects. Don't even listen, cut and dethatch its best when you start to feel an inkling of attack. Ask for a stronger shield and you are in the firing line at times, and nobody or anything will harm you. Rest in our safety. This days you understand and know more, it's all up to your training and hard work. At times you have asked why but that was part of your promise before you where reborn once again, for more work. The life itself is a universal school of opportunities and exams. Go ahead with confidence and heal and encourage. Many are searching and have so for years. It's hard to know where the truth lies and where to go. Too many say they have the truth maybe so a little bit of the whole picture, but study and wait learn more. It's a pattern so stand back and ask for more information. Blessings and love from all of your helpers, teachers and sages.

Love forever. TttA

TO BE CALM IS TO BE STRONG!

Let our guiding light and wisdom go with you throughout the whole day. Plenty of work is waiting for you so get ready. Many are in such turmoil because of the shifting and change with the whole universe. Most does not believe what's going on and try to explain in a scientific way. That's human but remembers who is in charge. We are the only ones that know the full story. Manipulation and mind control is appearing everywhere, so beware. Stay alert and let the forces of nature aid you in you quest. The last few days has been very challenging. Many working for the light have been attacked and disturbed. Guide and support each other until the dawn breaks. Most conditions at present are temporary. So wait until clearing is given. We are aware of all your agendas and work. Once again we say leave it to us and surrender. We are watching over you and your work, rest assured that is so.

Eternal love and joy. TttA

CONFESSION TIME!

Always have a clear slate when possible. At times it will take effort and some time when we say wait a little. Wait, It's for a reason when we say so and other events are sometimes a reason to stop for a while. Other people involved might not be in a state of understanding or circumstances have altered. Just ask us when and how. We know how the level of growth is and how some try to do their best. Remember not to do anything to please someone else what you feel is right for you to do at that time. Free will still exist. No one should ever influence except when being asked for input. Mind control is one of the biggest down falls for mankind. So many use the ego as an important source. To feed the ego does not give anyone peace. The human conditions are geared to use ego in many businesses. Change is needed to be on the agenda to enable all to get a better life and to grow. Freedom of actions, thoughts and spirit is very much a great reality and help.

Courage and love. TttA

LOOK AT YOUR CONNECTIONS!

Have another look at your dealings with others. For a

time it seems to be OK but later it's not genuine. It will be the true person coming out, also look at signs and situations taken for granted. If and when we say tell others to do so. Then it's up to them to make a decision. Time and time again you are doing just that. Be a courier and still we say look where it's all coming from. Many have gifts and don't use them, such a waste. Someone else will then take your place and the combination will not be the same. Carry out what is given to you the best way possible and we will do the rest. Many new believers of our work will open their hearts and minds to the truth as we want, and we want you to stay patient. We are speaking to their hearts and if and when think we will send them to you or someone with like mind in true spirit. It's a chain of connections and work teams that will strengthen the course for the good of all mankind. Stay detached and joyful when possible. Don't tread where angels fear to go. Blessings and balance from us all.

We are on target. TttA

WORK AND REST!

Let that advice be present in your life. A balance that we often have talked about. It might seem to be only a repetition but it is very valid for most growth in spirit mind and body. Never underdo or overdo anything especially when time is of essence. When stress or tired nerves are apparent. Stop and rest no tired spirit can do work of value for the universal force. We are thankful for help and taken advice from so many light workers and at times you feel it hard to decide, wait and ask us for a clear line. Now people have been coming prompted by us to unite. Wait a little longer and more will come. It all takes time to get ready. Expect miracles and miracles will come. Patience and silence is its always work done in the unseen and the result comes later. There is a plan with it all. Thank you for being available when we prompted you.

Go in peace my child. TttA

DEAL ONLY WITH TODAY!

Please do just that. You get on better when you don't mingle or mix anything or anyone, at the same time. To save time and money follow through our teachings. All energy needs to be centred and used in a positive way. So much and so many would like to have a percentage or a meal ticket as you say on Earth. Many of your sayings help you to remember when we walked on the Earth plane. We had parables. Some have trouble with readings so remember so a picture served the purpose better. All that is just tools and we have given you them to spread the message. All other tools that we have been given you also a heathy reminder to look after them well. We are backing you up fully because your work needs to be evenly distributed. Only eat when required and remember the water. As your system is still altering go easy on yourself. Say no when you feel tired. Recharge and rest is O.K. The weather is also affecting you so don't push anything if you are uneasy. It's around you, wait its O.K. to do nothing.

Courage and love from us all. TttA

PATIENCE AND JOY!

Thus two areas go hand in hand. When you stop and think you will understand to get joy you would be wise to be patient. Divine timing is on the agenda once more. Joy but humans act very often in haste so the result will not be the same. We know how often and how easy it looks at times but still and quiet times will lead you to glorious joy like a trusting child that is led by a parent's guiding light. Rebellion and impatience will lead you to wrong decisions. Let the day unfold in its own good speed. You have now seen more of respect work and new connections calling to you so you can see it's a plan for you and the only thing you needed to do was surrender and leave it to us. Trust and good work is increasing so you can see we are around you. Tomorrow comes soon enough sure to see us.

Glory to God Amen. TttA

PASS THE GOOD NEWS ON!

Yes, you will not get any more wisdom if you don't give out what we have given you. The light is not meant to be hidden in a dark place but a light could easily lighten up darkness and dismiss the shadows. We have been giving you light, love and wisdom for many years and we are happy with your work you are doing. More is to come and you will have more connections at dawn. Let that encourage you and keep you on the path. Life goes on and every new day you are greeting us at dawn. Let that encourage you and keep you on the path of enlightenment. Let the day enrich you and support your spiritual work. The load at times has been very heavy and you have finally learnt to hand it over to us at night. Surrender means surrender. Yesterday's lovely surprise was reward for work and it also lifted your spirit. The outcome will be better your cares are given to us to deal with. Blessed be in rich measure and let today be a day of joy, cheer and information.

From the eternal team TttA

THIS IS A NEW DAY!

Yesterday is gone to learn from and to understand it was best what was not happen. At times you will see clearly and other times a little more dim. Let go of uncertainties and trust us fully as you have seen that many alterations and events are changing around you. The question comes why and what is the next chapter. It's not written yet, so wait and listen in. Things and people are still getting sorted. It's out of your hands now so don't dwell on it. We have your best interest at heart so believe trust and persevere. It's a long hard lesson in the beginning but you are on your way with many years of new input of tools and people for the next group is being worked at and it might seem odd at times but bear with it. You are doing what's on your path. Today is another time and place. Go with it and we are supporting you as always with the clearing and changing. Yesterday has renewed the energies around you and yours. Look up and see how we will show you some signs.

Blessings and love. TttA

CARRY ON AS YOU HAVE STARTED!

Let this first month be a good start of the year. Many of you have had thoughts about change, or get a change to look at things a little deeper in to life and see what life is all about for you, taking stock and seeing the reality of it all. It takes time but all good work does. To build a strong fort or a lasting stronghold will take some planning from your architect. The main plan or your blueprint is being presented to you and it's up to you how you are dealing with it. Stand aside and be an observer. Emotional involvement is fine in the right combination but don't make any decisions at that time. A clear head and a willing spirit is essential. Another week soon gone and work is being done even if you don't see it at first but we do. Carry out your daily tasks and don't look to far ahead. Surrendering is still the big word for the day and every day. The alterations are on their way.

Love, laughter and loyalty. TttA

KEEP UP YOUR ORDER!

Let nothing or no one keep you from your order, most of all your spirit work. We do know when your moments of delay or time just goes. Tell us and we will be back. Enjoy our meetings and learn from our joined energies. Go on today with vigilance and unfolding. You already know when its divine timing it will work out the best way possible. Life is moving along slowly at times. There's a reason for that. Checking and double checking is best. Protection is also of value. Think and ask and it will be done. Claiming is stronger and see it before its happening. All is ground rules and very valid. As you go along on your path let's go together and enjoy. The new spiritual unfolding is ongoing and eternal. Learn from us and beware of some misguided souls that think they know unintentionally but still not right. Most people want power and attention so at times all methods are used. Understand but do not follow and let the light spread upon your face and spread it out.

Blessed be. TttA

FRESH START!

Let the day be a first day of your life. Hope for solutions and healing of spirit, mind, body and emotion. So much depends on your decisions and how fast you can see and hear. Stand back once again and get high up and look down on the situation. You will get a better over view and see quite clearly what's going on. Act accordingly and act with the universal principles. Go ahead with work today and enjoy little surprises and guide and support others. Many new connections will come and sit and just be. The wants of people are different so ask us for the best answers for that person that we have sent to you. You are still being trained so listen encourage and help if we say so. Thank you for your assistance and we are giving you all of your tools, practical help and uplifting. Rest after and say all is well in good working order. Bless all living things and send out love and light in big measure to aid the universal creation. Thank you once again.

We are giving so you can do your living. TttA

BALANCE!

Let go of the little interruptions. It was only a test once again. You are now handling things better than before, also more receptive to our guidance and help. We are rejoicing with you for that. Carry on as you are doing your part so we can give you more to work with. Many are trying to tell you how, what and when they do, don't listen. Only good advice is meant as such but they have not got the experiences of your life. No one can really understand if they have not felt it themselves. Good try but not deep enough. Have understanding and compassion. One day more and you will understand where you come from, talk less and listen more and you will know where they are or who sent them.

Care wisdom and love from all your teachers and healers..

Blessed be! TttA

STAY CENTRED IN OUR ENERGY!

To be able to stay calm, balanced and grateful whatever happens is a gift from us. You remembered to ask us this time. So all went much better. At last you have found out who is behind the masks of some people. Nothing that is not genuine can't stay good and growing. Reality is what's true and honest. So many are being exposed and so many situations cleared up. That is a part of life so that's why it is so important to say from your heart how you feel and what is the motive. Most people have been so programmed from all sorts of sources so they never stop and only a few have started to make up and see a bigger picture. Everyone's journey is a very special travel to many events and experiences. Take notice and learn from it. Follow your instinct and do what's right for you. Many will try to convince or alter your ways. That is not up to them. You are the only one that is responsible for actions and thoughts.

Breath of life and energy from the stars. TttA

RAIN AND SUNSHINE IS A PART OF THE SHIFT!

The planet Earth has been going through so many changes and still much more to come. The photon belt is activated and this time will never come again. Take notice and follow through as much as possible. Let the order that you now have assist you in the progress. Ask for a clearer picture and we will explain to you so you can pass it on. Your technology is not advanced enough as yet. So we will translate in your terms. So you can understand faster. We are doing what we can to protect, assist and to some of you. Too much knowledge in the wrong hands could be wrongly used to the down fall of many. Tonight is meeting time again. Ask and you will receive all that you have asked for and more. We have your best interest at heart many wants proof so we are showing signs and events to aid the trust and progress as travelling companions for your growth upwards.

Many blessings and thanks for your listening. TttA

SPREAD OUT THE GOOD ENERGY!

Yes my child you are doing just that, but not to fare for too long. Work needs to be done. But you are not yet qualified to do all of it as we have pointed out so many times only do what you can at your level. You are studying and learning as fast as you can so keep up your discipline and programs. It all will take time so don't be concerned over not being able to do all in a day as you want. Many tasks are daily so do as many tasks that cannot wait. The main thing is to balance all four parts of you out so not one area suffers. We still are staying close by and you know that so call us. Last night's session went extra well due to combined effort from all. You don't have to know in details what's going on that are not your business. You are holding the energy and cooperating as we have asked you. Everything is going according to plan, so enjoy the rest of the day. You will hear about the missing out later.

Onwards and upwards. TttA

ORDER!

Let our teachings uplift, support and be a guiding light on your path. Climb up and enjoy the view. The cooperation in your kind of work is not coming at present time. All seem to work on their own agenda. That is an ego trip and you would do best to listen and join forces. We are giving all life force and all other aspects as you require. Remember you are not the architect only the builder. That's important too. But remember who your teachers are. Also keep in mind to follow through and empty out. Before you receive more from us. Many wonder why nothing new is given that is why we are reminding you to think about it and how can anything more fit in when there is no room. Go ahead with today's unfolding and enjoy what you can. Listen and take note. Many mean well but have not got the whole picture and give out advice that is not suited. So many times we have said that to you. The dosage must suit the person because you are on different paths and levels.

Love and light. TttA

POSITIVE THINKING!

Let no one change your positive ideas, work or communication. Let your spirit flow and let life take a leap into the next chapter. You are going through a time of rethinking, relooking and researching. You are questioning why at times, and you are understandingly doing so. Human conditions are so involved and tangled, so it takes time to sort out, and when we say wait, then wait. It's not yet time for so many areas and it is not yet time for bigger changes. You are dealing with so many areas at the same time, so go easy on yourself. One day at a time still goes. It is getting sorted with our help and your cooperation. Don't concern yourself with too many practical details, go with the flow and leave it to us. We know that you need to be or want to be in good a shape as possible for your work and life in general. We are making it as easy as we can for you. Carry on with your day as we have given you help joy and wisdom in full measure. Rest assured that all is indeed well. You are fully understood and protected.

Blessings and love. TttA

ASK US TO EXPOSE NEGATIVITY!

We are giving you lessons about sort outs and how to expose unwanted entities. Many of you have seen, heard and come across many situations with enemy vibrations that do not make you feel at ease or feel uncomfortable. If or when you feel that, stop at once and leave us to deal with it and clean it up. No good work can be done when you are disturbed. Good work will be done when the energies are combined and working towards the same goal. Unity is very valuable also to speak up when not understood. Plain speaking is also advisable. Let today unfold in a best possible way It's not to ignore you only to protect you. People that have been kept away from you is a lesson in our way to teach you. The exposure was for your own good. Let today be just that. Carry out today the tasks which have been given and do something for yourself.

Blessings in rich measure. TttA

BEWARE AND WATCH OUT!

To be able to trust is hard when so many have played games and they really think they are getting away with it. No one does and all will be dealt with in due course. Leave them all to us, otherwise you will use too much energy and time to find the right way to deal with them. No you have seen how low some people can get. Many are not in control of themselves, so not enough attention is given to their actions. Also many are misinformed about you and who you really are. Today will prove to be a different day. Leaving for a recharging and be able to stay apart and see a little better. Who is who? It's too easy to get too close to something or someone. That will always cloud your picture. Detach and cut strings that have nothing to do with you. Compassion is still fine but people are looking for a quick fix. Tell them it does not work that way. Groundwork and a stable foundation. Life is here to teach you and learning lessons long overdue.

Courage and peace. TttA

THE ANSWERS ARE COMING!

Many times you have been asking just that and that is understandable, but solutions take time. The conditions needs to be as perfect as possible. Don't act to soon otherwise it will not compute. Very many conditions and people lacking of knowledge is often the blockage. Try to do it as we see it. We have a clearer picture seeing everything from above. The same goes for your learning. Today you asked again and we told you so. Everything went well. It was a lot of information given and good will. People that're not respecting the time situation are being exposed though it's not to every body's liking, but it still helps. When you are looking back you can see why and also get another lesson learnt. Many more will come this year. Leave that to us. You don't need to remind or call. It's not up to you. Do what's on your plate and follow through. We know that you know it's only a reminder my child of light. Thank you for your work last night. We will let them know who you are.

Blessings TttA

GODS SPEED!

This last few days you have been exposed to a lot of adverse circumstances. Surprise surprise how many expose themselves Detach from then it would, it would be a loss of time and good energy. Keep on dealing with this tangled web we know that you know so wait and let us deal with the operation. Trusting and testing has its purpose but enough is enough. We do know what's been thrown at you. We have done what we were able to soften the blow. Others will come instead of just hangers on. Everyone is given a chance to grow if idleness takes place leave them to it. You have had a deeper look how to recognise implants and take over.

You don't have to ask us as you already know otherwise. Don't say if you are not asked. Other forces are at work so information about you somebody would love to have. If you feel uneasy keep quiet or work away. Protection is given.

Love and light. TttA

AT LAST!

You have heard us earlier on and you got carried away. Control your doings and focus on your priorities. Words always interest you how and what it all means. That is a subject you like but first do your orderly promised tasks. Well now we are so busy now, so work on doing all when we meet you every day. Last night was very beneficial for all also for once that was not with you in the physical. The light went very far away oversees too many souls. We know that you can see with your inner eye exactly what went on. Our request this morning, you did something about it and it will bear fruit. Universal but not possible. We know best so listen in carefully and calmly. Always empty out and stay ready to receive. By now you know our order that's needs to be followed. It's only a practise for you at this point. Keep your discipline up and you are being cherished and taught ancient wisdom. Lots of care love and joy from your team.

Love and light. TttA

WEAR YOUR CLOAK!

It's time to go out in public in a protection cloak or whatever you have chosen to use. Still beware of today's many disguises. Many are just so subtle and cunning so it's hard to believe that anyone could try to deceive you. Well now we know that you are able to spot the money. Enough of this kind of talk. The work is still going on and will be always, so stay vigilant and keep on learning. It's all in the melting pot so leave all with us. Too many areas are affected and it's not wise at this time to move on any work subject too fast. Waiting and patience are two good standbys for now. Beware of what people bring and what their eyes look like. Checking is very essential for now. In the waiting time do only the most essential. Take care of not overdo anything. All is under control, only believe and trust. Relax and enjoy the rest of your day. Be outside as much as possible and use the nature forces.

All our love, light and support from your loving team. TttA

LET THERE BE LOVE!

We are reminding you today about love, eternal and lasting. The universal kind is the best and moist beneficial, but the human kind is also our love sent in to you on Earth. Love is unselfish and never wanting something in return. If and when it comes it's a bonus. Give out love and love will come back to you, not always the way you think. Many times you might not recognise it. Think carefully and check out which source was the beginning. Always ask if you don't know. Our love goes to all living things and that is a very big part of healing and recharging .The expression of love takes many forms actions, words and thoughts, and many more similar areas. Let today be a day of communication and cooperation. The ones that come to your door are still sent by us, so it is for different purpose, but all for a connection with the light. The ones that have negative thoughts will be dealt with by us.

Love and light from the highest order. TttA

BLESS THE LIFE IN YOU!

Bless each day as it starts. Bless the life that you have been given. So many opportunities and so much blessed work to be done and has been done. Nothing gets forgotten and everything is written down in the book of your life. Lessons to be learned and understood. Not many have understood that. Listen in carefully and take note. We have explained to you many times how it all works, so practise and practise again. It will take time but time is eternal, so use it in the best way as possible, if not benefitting you let it go. Many tasks are time consuming and could easily be a controlling factor, in anyone's life. If not sure how much time ask and remember the word balance. Too much

judgement. Beware of too much on looking that's when you should think about balance. You of all people have worked on that for some years now. Keep doing so for a while longer you just feel when things are all out. Stop and do something about it. Ask us for input and still surrender each morning and leave all things to us to sort out. Eagerness is fine when you have a positive goal but otherwise leave it alone. Much good work will not be done if you are trying to do it yourself, not having enough information about the subject. Last night was beneficial for all the ones that did not come missed out and that is none of your business. Cut and detach after every connection which was draining and energy was depleted. You came back to us and got recharged Use your crystals and do your connection never get unplugged from us.

Blessings in many ways. TttA

PEACE IN THE STORM!

That is one of the requirement for inner peace that is what you all can use when the natural forces are telling you about the interferences with the Earth and its resources. Leave all natural oil and coal it's necessary for mother Earth to let them work for the planet. Still keep on sending love and light to the whole universe. Every little input is vital and you already know how to heal the earthly conditions. We all need all light workers to act as a chain of light all around the planet. That will activate what's already there and stop all infiltrations from outer space. We have noted lately how many are tired and doubtful about our actions. Understandable but all is in working order. As you asked for signs you got them and quite many facts also. What you don't see you are not ready for. In the stillness of the morning you feel the connection with us much stronger. Let's enjoy today together and let it all unfold in divine order and time. Talk and trust us for further news, its coming.

Blessings and love. TttA

INFORMATION FROM THE STATION!

Yes my children of light you are becoming a good clear channel for us. To pass on and to do your kind of work takes time energy and discipline, and you have plenty of that now. Keep some and get the balance right to give out certain percentage. No stagnation in our kingdom and in your lives. Let the inflow and outflow bring you love and light in full measure. You also know about expressions expectations and acceptance. What you cannot change you need to accept and leave the conditions to us. We have said so many times that deep and grave situations would be too much to deal with on your own. Rest assured that all is in working order. Let the day unfold as it makes your place always a target. Because of your work we will send extra guards to you so you can work on undisturbed. Your Orion connection is very disturbed. He will be restrained and healed in our time. Keep up your assignment and more is coming to you. All you have to do is prepare your home and yourself. Remember to do nothing at times. Recharging time. Thank you.

More tomorrow. TttA

ABIDE IN ME!

The white eternal light is inside you, so no one or nothing can interrupt or try to convince you any more about others truths. You do know how most of your connections operate. Don't try to alter their beliefs or tell them if they are not getting the yes from us. People are wondering about timing and why the turmoil. Well, as you know it's all about the changes and together with the photon belt's operation twelve long years to be in a sort out mood, but some situations are so complex and others tangled. Relationships tasted and dislikes are all in for a major upheaval. You have studied that for some years now and many more years to come. Keep up your discipline and focus. For you it has been a huge transformation of spirit mind and body and emotions. It has taken a big toll but it was necessary for the work you still are doing for yourself and others. Be still and know that I am God. Rest and relax to go in to your special place of peace and tranquillity.

Joy and eternal life. TttA

OPEN YOUR MIND, BODY AND SOUL TO THE LIGHT AND LOVE!

By receiving and giving out you will never get any stagnation, of any areas in your life. That will in turn make a strong growth and get your life to see and experience many new things. Today you have had another revelation. That was good and helpful. Get in touch with us many more times of the day. Stay very close and all will be well. At present time you are experiencing many thoughts, feelings and new ideas. Understand that was necessary for growth and to help others on their way to a higher place. Go on your way to see, hear and smell the scent of heaven. We are standing very close to you because of the changes in awareness. It's coming very fast so take a break in between to catch up in some areas. We also are aware of your connections all or nothing the egg shape. When the egg has hatched you will see clearer. The two new tools are coming soon.

Blessings and love from us all. TttA

EARLY MORNING SUN!

Take on board all that warmth and rays from the sun that will benefit you in winter days to come. You already know about the spirit bank. To store away for days to come is to prepare and stay practical. Many tasks are still time consuming but you are learning to be more flexible. Every day that goes by you will see more and more how rich the universe is, and you only have to ask us. The storehouse is ours to give when we choose to. The plants and animals are also feeling the shifts and they don't know is happening so they act strange and confused. Look at the nature and listen to the winds. This time of the day you have a change to tune in and the picture much clearer. We share with you all through the night and a lot of work was done for your benefit and ours. You know by now that you needed to go a lot deeper with your thoughts and stay firmly connected to us. Don't ever get unplugged. You are forever in our midst and very welcome wherever you go. One day you will notice the increase of awareness of people. It is a good sign. It's also waking up to life.

Always yours. TttA

ADVANCEMENT!

Let's talk about what you can do to advance in all areas. First of all ask us to put your spirit in charge and then all others will follow. When the connection is there use it. Well now advancement is very beneficial and will aid you and all you come across to be closer connected to the source. Open your mind, spirit and body to the eternal knowledge and light. Empty out and you will receive. The pattern is very important and also helps you to keep things in order. When you have mastered the first as what we gave you the next step is to add some knowledge and open your eyes to see the connection between the universe and the solar system that you live in. It is only a small part that is known to you so expand your thoughts further away. When visiting us at night you are getting your knowledge and specific tools to aid and save time and energy. Preprograming has played a big part in your life. Well-meant but not always useful. Others cannot walk on your path so keep all good and discard the rest, so more input can be given about the big picture.

Blessings and love. TttA

REFRESHMENT DAY!

To be able to refresh when life is getting a little dull is indeed a gift from heaven. To alter little things might be enough to alter the look of the whole area. Also we want you to look at life from a different viewpoint. That will shed some light into a few unexplained situations. Maybe you will just turn things upside down or facing the east. Also use copper that has a beneficial effect on many that are influenced by nature. Music also plays a big part of healing in all areas. Remember they are all tools, and you should treat them as such. When your work grows and advances you will be given more tools. Keep an open mind about tool changes so you know how it is to be a sign from us. This wonderful season is about to change to autumn and that is another reason to do more balance work inside and out. It's all in seasons to help you to do what you want. Priorities are still important so give that some thought. Your garden is also a big part of your sanctuary a safe haven for many wounded souls.

Blessings. TttA

LET'S JUST BE TOGETHER!

Togetherness is a good way to exchange and revitalise. Only remember who you do it with. Your work is in cooperation with ours and a good exchange. Little links in a big chain of protection work and healing is activated. Think what happen when one link breaks the whole line will be out of order and give the Negative forces an entrance. Stay strong and very flexible. To bend when the storm comes is fine you soon bounce back again. A big strong root system and years of training would help you to know which degree you can go to. Study the trees and feel their life force. Touch the trunk and branches and talk to the living nature. It will respond. Some might tell you about water, wind or Earth it would have seen throughout the years. Sit under a healthy tree and recharge. Two kinds of growth, one under and one above. Time out.

Enjoy today! TttA

CLEARING AND JOY!

To clear the pipeline is essential; you can't do much when the line is clogged up. Many odd and strange things are occurring. Don't take any notice just carry on with tasks that need to be done. Animals and all living things feel the change in the air and don't understand why. Confusions and wrong timing is all about change. That is a part of the alterations. Preparations for the half turn so work is being done to make it possible to happen. Your whole is very busy and thousands of others have their hands full of connecting work. Let this be a time of advent. Look at so many people needing road signs. They don't know if they are coming or going. Late last night you got one more sign that the manipulations are everywhere. That was no news to you, but still you got a reminder. Let us guide you and your actions the best way as possible for you. Understanding and growth. Keep smiling and focus on something most of the day. Forever in your thoughts.

Love and light from us all. TttA

TRUST AND BELIEVE!

When you hear these words you can take it as a sign that you need to do just that. We do know where you are and don't think for a moment that we have forgotten you. Today you experienced another helpful time in cooperation with the source. Take the golden opportunity when it feels right. It was very beneficial and you did connect fast and well with us the eternal source. Our storehouse is full of all the provisions that you require. Back again to have 100% trust and believe. Leave all others and all jobs to be finished by us. Don't ever try to do that by yourself. It will take a very qualified spirit to see the whole pattern. Be vigilant when to act quick actions is only good when spirit suggests. To be able to hear and see is an advanced teacher-student situation. So many forget to check they are plugged in so the message gets infiltrated.

Blessings. TttA

ABIDE IN ME!

Rest and work in that order and all will be well. This morning proved just that. Preparations are very important most of the planning you can confidently give to us, and the only part that is for you to do. Rely more and more on our support, love and wisdom. You have been working harder to be in tune with us and our pattern, so keep that up. You are still uneasy at times but lesser than before. The trust, joy and health are playing a part in your new life for the source. Your commitment is great so please stay with us. Sometimes you get tired and rightly so. Stop at once and after a break you soon get the energy back again. People in general terms either like you or dislike you that is for you to check and you will know straight away which side they belong to. Why would anyone try to daunt you such a waste of time. You have been smiling many times when you have seen what's going on. Keep up the good work.

Thank you. TttA.

REJOICE!

Yes my child of light rejoice, in so many ways you are a very fortunate person. You have had years of learning and education about the spirit world. At times you have not fully understood the meanings of our teachings, but you are getting a glimpse of our world. Keep on doing what you are and learning something more every day .To add on knowledge is to grow and evolve. It's never too late to learn more. The inspiration must come from the positive light if not you will not get a good result. Ask for it and it will come to you when required. Perhaps you might think that was not how I would have liked it. God is always right on time. Focus on us and our storehouse is very well supplied. How much many more would benefit from that. They only have to ask us. Always look at the source of someone's advice and also remember to look at their eyes. You don't have to say anything only look. Be glad and others will be so with you also. Thank for being a good and faithful servant of the universal spirit and light.

Blessings and light for the day. TttA

CARRY ON REGARDLESS!

At times you wonder why things are not moving but as you know it's not the right time as yet. Many alterations are a foot, and you will do well just to go with the flow, for now. Last night was very good the ones that found other things to do just missed out. Anyway that is not your concern. Keep on doing as we have suggested. The universe is a big place and so much is going on to follow the sort out and all the preparations for a better world. If and when you don't hear or see anything- wait. We know how things are for you many times. You have learned privacy, patience and posture. We do know how much energy and time it has taken. New input will come so make a new list. To be flexible and practical is good. You will have answers and get more clues. Always look for the good in all as we do and still earn from every situation. Life is a big school time with homework and lessons. Watch out who you follow. Loving and happy thoughts be with you today and forever.

Your teachers and healers. TttA

TRY AND TRY AGAIN!

Forever trying will get you there. So much for such a long time get you a little weary. When that feeling comes stop and rest. Recharging is very essential now, not because of age only the kind of work you are doing. Help will come from unexpected sources. Trust and enjoy something every day. Look at the plant life, how it grows in seasons and what rain and weather does. There again all living things need balance. Soak up every sunny ray and the energy from your garden. Simple things are always the best and often the best things take less effort. Today's events will prove to be rewarding. Ask us for the right time and environment. Stay and stand back until all O K is given, so much is up to how you act and receive from us. To follow through is very important. It's like a school of wisdom with homework. The new projects you have will be very useful. Keep up the good work and do have spell between jobs. All the colours in your garden will help and keep you in our care.

Love, light and wisdom. TttA

GREETINGS!

Once again we meet, talk and exchange. Let that be a time of renewal. We also need you as much as you need us. Forever exchanging and giving out love, light and healing. That is why you are here at night to get a refill of all that you want and need for your work on Earth. It's been many years and you have learnt a lot. In some areas it has taken longer to accept our wisdom, but you are still human, and you are not yet complete in our way of thinking. Still do your best and fulfil others as you have been taught. The eternal wisdom passed on to others make the whole thing flow. Let today encourage and heal you. It's hard at times to fully grasp all the truth. Life has dealt with you very severely, but it had to be. At times you see very clear what's going on, but the timing is not yet to be as it looks to be. Be patient and do what you feel is right for now. This time is still a preparations time, so sort out what next that you feel called to do. Your requirement is not what others will have, but you already know that.

Blessings and love. TttA

ONWARDS AND UPWARDS!

One step at a time gets you to your goal. At times you don't feel it's going fast enough but it is still going. To be able to see and hear what's going on in the pattern of life is indeed a gift. Treasure that and build on it as no one's path is exactly the same. The quest is for all to do and fulfil lessons learned from us and to be used in life. We do know how things are. The human race is beginning to take a stand so work on that all of you. Progress will be made slow at first, but still it is progress. Keep alert and aware and highly intuitive. It will take some work, but you can do it. There is still a lot of that which needs answers, so deal with them one at the time. Life could be a lot easier if you only see listen and hear sooner. Be ever ready to listen, but first empty out and stay calm, peaceful and serene. Basic rules for groundwork and the law of our teachings still stand.

Keep going as you are for now. More work is coming so prepare yourself. Your visit last night was very beneficial.

Yours forever. TttA

KEEP FOCUSING!

Let no one or nothing stop you to focus on your work first. Other areas need to be kept an eye on also. Priorities and order is very valid. Many old connections are close now. The most valuable ones are getting closer. Others will try. Watch out for the ones that think they know it all. That is not very spiritual and most of the times they have been neglected so they feel they need to speak up everywhere. Human conditions are so complex at times. Most don't stop and think just carries on as many generations done before. Many ideas still have value but others have lost their validity. Times are changing so fast so you feel that time is speeding up. You are right it is! The first thought that comes in to your mind is the right one, only ask us first. Wrong advice at this time is dangerous. If not clear guidance is given wait until the O K from us. Go easy on yourself and let the day unfold as best as possible. The Earth is on the move again- the new path is emerging in the orbit.

Blessings and courage. TttA

SURRENDER!

Please do so as there is too much unease and discomfort at present. Don't get carried away or fooled by it. Check and follow your gut feeling. It will take a very strong faith and courage to see through all the disguises and subtle ways of the opposition. How well trained they are. Use your training to advance and get on with your quest. Beware of feelings and happenings that interfere in your area of life. Life is going on and it is up to the individual to look and give your actions much thought. Last night and early this morning you got proof again of deception and misinformation. It was exposed for what it was and dealt with. It was quite cruel and negative. You know who was doing that to you. Someone only wants energy and go to the light and they finally did. So many negative souls are waking up from a bad dream and want to change. You are the one they come to. To be able to send all these souls to the light with our help is not an easy task, but you are trained.

Love, light and joy for today TttA

IN THE STILLNESS OF THE MORNING!

Begin with the stillness to be able to recharge and invigorate you. Many times you have begun in another manner. Circumstances are forever changing so it takes time and things will not move before all the involved people are there. That is why you wonder why you are ready but keep on learning about patience all have to do and live their pattern, so the combination of people in your life seeking you of levels of understanding and acceptance. Beware of hurrying things along only in an emergency, as spirit will prompt you. Unfolding time and caution must be in your mind. Only do your tasks as required. Life goes on and you can't stop the current ebb and flow. Stand back and look a little closer at the pattern. At present time it's too easy to forget and not keep your order. Beware of side trackers. If and when you are not sure wait a little. Unfolding time and sorting out is still present. Let today be a day of joy, restoration with a positive outlook. Blessings from the highest.

Love, light and wisdom. TttA

SEE THROUGH OUR EYES

Try to see what the purpose of life is. Quite often you look with human eyes, and now you are trying very much to see what the real picture is. Don't be discouraged in what you see, but only ask us to expose the situation so you can easily look at it and make a decision. Today's news was expected, and you already knew the answer. Well now that's good. Always wait and let us confirm. Trust is building up so keep up the good work. More information will come today. Wait, even if you don't hear. Timing at present is crucial. Keep on smiling and trusting, and say all is well.

By doing so you draw positive people and actions to you and that will increase yours. Focus and keep occupied and things will be moving. You all are feeling the uncertainty and wonder why you will be shown a picture and other signs. Patience will be rewarded and every day is a new day, so start afresh. Events are on the move so bade your time. In the meantime carry on as usual. The sun will break through.

Everlasting love and light. Conquer in our name.

Love and light TttA

ONLY BELIEVE!

Well now that might sound simple and when interruptions and events occur as an alarm there's a very good reason for it all. When you come in to that situation only surrender and believe. All is really in good working order when you don't understand or see it its often harder wonder or disbelief. Throughout so many years of lessons and learning you have seen wonders unfolding. Keep on with your work and spread the good wisdom. Some think it's you but you know very well it's through you. You are still the scribe and light worker so keep going in that knowledge that you are. The group work is only a little part of your energy work. People that pick or are trying to put you down should have a good look at themselves and it's only their or a host living in them that wants to daunt you. All it is doing is making you stronger and wiser. Let go of the ones that not responding or listening. Enjoy today and stay very firm in your convictions. All is as it should be. More work is being activated.

Blessings and love from us all. TttA

PAYBACK TIME!

That is what we have said. Groundwork and follow through is of most valuable importance. You have seen so many times how much work has been done in the name of the light and love. At times it will take more time, but that is not for you to deal with. Leave all that very advanced work to us. It would take too much of your energy to deal with it. Later on when you have advanced higher you will get more of higher evolved work. For now you follow through what we give you each day. This morning you got another proof that we are very close to you, wherever you go and you are very well looked after. It was a test once again and you passed. Let the rest of the day be used as a catch up time and stay close to us. Last night was very peaceful and all others benefitted from it. One day more will come we will sort that out. You met one soul again this morning. It was important that you follow through our guidance.

Blessed be our friend and worker. TttA

ONWARDS AND UPWARDS!

Carry out our work that is the pattern of the day, and times to come. We are looking to improve your life in all areas. You have started to feel the difference. Wonders are unfolding and you will be pleasantly surprised when they come. Believe only believe it's so simple. We have told you so for years but we are now reminding you again. It's important that you fully grasp the whole connection and the bonds that are being strengthened. Work and rest is part of the pattern so look at is such. The season is changing again when you look at the leaves turning golden and many plants have done their season. Later on other plants will be replaced and others renewed. That is a part of the pattern also. Believe yourself and the great universal force are very well bound together. Links that cannot be broken and all the force and energy is coming through to you from us. Keep up what you are doing and we will do the rest.

Glory to God in the highest .AMEN. TttA

ANOTHER DAY ANOTHER START!

Keep going as you are. Plenty of work for the light that is universal. The Earth is only a little part of it all, but valuable. The last time we spoke you got a little more information. It all adds up to a big picture and it would help you and others to know and to make the connection. Many times when you think you got more of the unfoldment and puzzle it's only a little part of the diamond. Anyway you still are working on your part of the improvement for all mankind peace moves will also alter. The same goes for life when you work on one aspect of your life it will alter the whole situation. In the times alone with us you are getting all the information you want for each day. It must come in chapter as all growth does. To learn one thing as the law requires will help you to the next chapter. That means to do your groundwork and have a steady base for your future work. Also it will help you to stay unbreakable when it storms around you. Be with us in the quite places and always go back there at night.

Love! TttA

BE A LIGHT AND LIGHT A LIGHT!

So much darkness and despair about. Don't get pulled in to it. Act as a light, no need to say or do anything. Just be and let us do the rest. It's still sort out time so in the meantime carry on as we direct. Patience and waiting time is still a very big part of your training. Many do not understand how many years it's taken to get where you are. Every lifetime has been a very big lesson. Some have not been accepted or fully understood, so the same lessons come back again and again, until all has been learned. Step out of yourself and rise high above it, then you will see what's going on. Being too close to anything or anyone could cloud your vision, so when you meet us again in the morning we support each other and exchange energy. The weekend's withdrawal is there for a purpose. You also got another look at life's mysteries. The phone call was there to alert you what's going on. Just keep going as you are. Trying times and time to grow. This week's meetings will surprise you. Let them come to you and you go to us.

Rich and warm blessings. TttA

ANOTHER MILESTONE!

Well now so many years and so much work has been archived. Still much more to do. Don't ever think that all the work has been done. It never will be, you only have to do and follow through what's yours and do it. Present situations are very tangled. Yesterday you had another confirmation of good result from a very tricky situation. Do your part and leave the rest to us. That is always the fastest way. Your curious nature makes you think at times "what next?" That is natural and we do understand. Leave all of the advanced solutions to us. You will be given the answers to your questions when you need them. Yesterday's joy was another connection again from so long time ago. You said what was on your mind and the bond got stronger. You will see one day soon. Let your life unfold naturally. Everyone has a different timeslot according to their system so be flexible and stay patient. Also remember how it used to be and learn from it as we know you are. Your combination highly tuned in and is different to many others so the balance wheel swings at times. Stay tuned in for today as it will bear fruit.

Eternal blessings from us all. TttA

CLEARING AND LIGHT!

To be able to see is a wonderful thing. When not clear or too dim, stop and clear and turn on the light. Light from the source and clearing of your line to them. At times it could be crossed wires or not plugged in. Many of the causes of not getting things through or not the whole message. When that occurs, wait and ask for a new channel or wait a while longer. So much is at present time wasting or getting side tracked. Watch out when unease is present. Stop and check if the N forces have started to panic again, so be on your guard. Outside in the sun is best to reach us. We know that you are very aware and alert others to the same picture. Let all others go that are not doing you any good or show you disrespect. Others are waiting and will come after the others have left. It's a standing unbending law of the universe. Cutting out dead wood is beneficial. Keep on getting through to us so many times you wish.

Lots of love and light. TttA

SO MUCH TO DO IN A SHORT TIME!

You don't have to do it yourself, only your part. The Earth is still in an uproar, and many of you are picking up the disturbances. To get inner guidance and peace in these times, you would do well to go in to your sanctuary to restore and get extra energy for times to come. It's not an alarming time but so much is going on in the unseen, so what you don't see is the clue. To work for the light you are protected at all times, not meaning that you are not in life to fight on a psychical level. Only stay very close and tuned in on a spiritual level. Your decision to cut off a few more connections was very valid. Your mind body and spirit is reacting to alien energy. These are your check points so stay with it. To survive is to stay firm in a way best possible. The war is not happening on a human level that so many of you have seen so much of lately. Watch out for spirit unrest and guard your entrance doors to other dimensions. At night most of your work is being done. So you really are working in two different places for the good of all mankind. Thank you.

Blessings. TttA

ENJOY THE MOMENT!

Remember to enjoy the little pleasures that we and others give you. That is to help to balance the picture and feel that all is well. Yesterday's event went well thanks to the co-operation. You are now more fully aware of the connection between us. For so many years you and I have worked and laboured to aid mankind. At the same time you have also helped yourself. So when one area is dealt with others will get more energy. It's all about connecting encouraging and learning. Speak your mind when you feel you should do so but keep quiet when rigid also. That is what we mean about to know when what or how things should be dealt with. Some days it's very much withdraw times other times its all go all day. The pattern is quite obvious. You have seen what's been happening. We have always said to you that you are not alone or unsupported. Time is always telling you what's what. Eastertime is coming with a nice feeling and events. Still we say one day at the time.

Remember the peace that filled your soul when you asked and it was an instant help.

Beware of unease. Blessings. TttA

KEEP GOING!

By doing just that you will get there. Pausing at times when you feel a thought of rest. No spirit that's tired will accomplish any good work for spirit. When you have your part stop and ask us to give you renewed strength and to take over. No need to think that you are not fulfilling your lessons and growth from it. People often think that they have to do it themselves. Not so love yourself and others with universal eternal love of the highest kind. The old way was to deny yourself and give all away of energy wealth and then less wanting for yourself and don't get it is not good for anyone. Love and honour yourself all are blessed in one way or the other. Give freely to others and yourself the same goes for taking rest and recharge. The equal part of love and light to all. When dark alien energy is present beware and stay clear. The unseen forces are on the warpath again. Leave all of that to us. Don't touch, surrender to us.

All our help healing and love. TttA

LET MY SUN SHINE UPON YOU!

The warmth and light from us and the planets give you all you want and require. Back to balance and how much to give out and what to keep. Many times you have been told just that. It's not an easy lesson. Beware of ego thoughts. Learn how to deal with it to be fair to all. That also includes you. Don't ever work to the limit, so stop and rest in between and then you can go ahead with renewed strength. Do your breathing exercises or sit in the sun. Listen to the wind and relax. Look at the tall trees and see how flexible they are, bending and not breaking. Let our wisdom engulf you and send away all others. So called know it all's. Enjoy something every day. Look forward to your goal and give yourself some credit. Encourage others also.so many are in deficit of love and light coming their way. Go with the changes and still stay close to us. The higher evolved work you do the closer the bond you are required to have. Only a request not an order.

Love and cheers from us all. TttA

LIVE AND LET LIVE!

Enjoy to just be, and understand that also has its purpose. Many times you think it's not for you and it's true. You don't belong in any ordinary quarters. A life set apart at the same time in your kind of work take many different turns. Think of it as an education towards your goal. You are advancing and growing and we have seen the work done in our name and you have learned to listen and hand over situations and pass on your knowledge. Later on you will see and hear more. It's all very gradual and rising up towards us. Try to be outside as much as possible every little bit helps and strengthen you for times ahead. Don't be alarmed only cautious of some people. Others have also noticed the connection to us and if and when they want tell them and give them to us. Tonight we will meet again in silence time. The best work is when you are relaxing meditating in silence. Don't forget to empty out and get ready to receive us. Let no one put asunder what has been built.

Love and laughter. TttA

ALL CLEAR!

The last few days you have been digging much deeper to get under the layers of disguise. Now you know about it all so that will make it much easier and less draining for you to give the ones that need your support more time and also will make you feel more at ease. Your system has been under a strain for the onslaught of others. They only wanted to have a meal on your energy. The exposure of the whole picture was a little brutal but now you know. Some of them also knew that you knew. We have looked at you and your life many times and now you understand how protected and guided you are. Your home is your sanctuary so the honest searching souls will come and sit and we will be there for you all. Let today be a day of thanks and recharging. Some are not aware of who is the master we will look after that side. The white light will enhance you and yours. Do what feels natural for the rest of the day. No forced actions. We know how much you are doing. Write a new list and feel good about it.

Blessings and joy from us all. Your request is being processed. TttA

DISCIPLINE!

One again we have met in spirit, but you have not written before today. I do know that you need quiet times to be able to focus. Give it a serious thought. Your life is changing again. So much to understand and look with detachment on what's happening around you it's all there for a purpose and needs to serve its course. The use of colour in your case is very beneficial and the sensitivity of yours might at times be very strong. Still wait for the right time before making any changes. Enjoy the time with others that are agreeing with you. We are fully supporting you in your work for the light. Still take time out and do nothing if you so choose. Enjoy the time with others that are agreeing with your life. Others that do not belong can go elsewhere that have nothing to do with you and leave it like that. Many are trying to discard or belittle you that is their loss. You know best what's going on because of your connection with us. For now stay silent as much as possible.

Care and love. TttA

ANOTHER GLORIOUS MORNING!

Let this day be something that you can draw from and remember how peaceful and calm it feels to be connected to nature and being a part of the force. Working to lighten up someone's path. Many walk in the land of the shadows and have done so for too long a time. If anything becomes a habit you pose and check so you can see what's going on. Beware of the system. Good discipline is called for and to focus on your goal. Never lose sight of your destiny, and still ask us when to rest and have a time out to recharge. Many light workers never have a break so they brake and don't have enough time on Earth to do it all that was prepared for them. Be wise and relax, smile and with poise. No good spirit work will be done from a tired spirit. That is to go against the mind. Naturally you feel guilty in the beginning so surrender your loved ones to us. We will still give you a part to do but you rob them of faith if you are telling or acting for them. Individuals are responsible for their own growth and can go to the source themselves. God's speed my friend.

Blessings for your work today. Our blessings. TttA

STEADY AS YOU GO!

To be able to stay calm and be in an observers position is very helpful at these times. Keep an eye on the people that come and go. They all have a purpose some more than others. It's not for you to decide what it is only let us use your home for this work that is needed to be activated. We will come and do what you have required or needs to be activated. Many areas that need to be sorted are above your knowledge so let us carry out what is our work. Today was another test for you and many ongoing actions come to light. Look at where it comes from and give thanks. The main thing was that you did not run away from it. Slowly and surely it all got done. Remember that we are around you and making sure you come through it all. Scares will go in time. Don't let any more appear. Lessons learned are to be remembered when you come across different situations. Inside work today will help and connect with us. Keep on connecting and relaxing. Stay safe in our midst.

Love and wisdom. TttA

BREAKING THROUGH!

My worker and friend you are doing just that. You were not fogged in only being in a land with different dimensions. Your extensive travel through the night has taken you to so many places and you met so many teachers and old friends. Your workload is the biggest of all life times because of your abilities and past experiences. Your beloved pets seem to follow you from so long ago. Always there for you and keeping you company. This time around you promised a lot and it is getting done but it is not for anybody. It takes courage and a lot of focusing to keep an eye on so many different areas and situations. We said we will give you examples, and so we are. Practise and then more practise. Many tangled and deep situations are being resolved for you and others. Stay patient and smile a little more. We do when we study you at times. You are trying your best, but you are doing it. Last week's confusions in the air is only a part of the universal changes and some do not know it yet but they will connect later.

Carry out today's task. More tomorrow. Stay close. TttA

EASTERTIDES!

Let the Eastertime be a time with new fresh start in spirit mind and body. New life and another look at your life. Enjoy the little gifts and glad surprises. Don't count in money only love from the heart. The heart is the centre of life and from that centre you can send lots of love and light in full measure. Make sure that the meaning of love and light from you and the source is pure and light. Warm up somebody's heart today or at least one or the one we send to you. Maybe for different purpose but that's not for you to decide. You are the builder we are the architects. It's all a cooperation still and working in all arias together. Remember when one aria is not well nor will the others. It's not true that you can treat one area and not the others. All cells are living cells so keep on sending them love and light. That will feed them all. Talk to your emotional and physical body, it's all a part of the chain. As the seasons are changing so will you. Warmest wishes for Easter and glad tidings.

Love and light. Carry out today's task. More tomorrow. Stay close. TttA

PREPARE FOR TOMORROW!

Get organised and look forward to a new start. Every year is different but still the same message is coming to you all gladness and Easter joy for the risen Lord. We are still watching over you and advising to what next. At times you would like to know ahead but trust us we are getting the supper table ready for a celebration of joy healing and warmth for many tired and frozen souls. Look closer to what and who is entering your place. We have promised to guard you and we are. Still you also involved in your work. Still a student and still growing. Well now it's taking time but time waits for no man. This Eastertime is different because of where the earth is placed in the planetary system. Bear with the changes and take one step at a time. We know how it has affected your physical system. Many do not know it but ailments unexplained are an effect of universal law and order. Your earthly law is changing from new thought pattern entering.

Love and courage. TttA

EASTER JOY!

Show the world love, light and compassion. The world of today is so in lack of genuine attitudes from people and animals. Disguise and mask wearing is flowering. Other masters are doing their best to mislead or disrupt light workers. Today Easter Sunday is a nice peaceful day let it stay that way and give cheer to so many as possible. Ask for what for each person and then leave it to us to deal with input from our wisdom from the ages. Relax and greet us when we come. You will get more benefit when that happens. The sun is there to warm and comfort you. The day will soon go and you will thank us once again for assistance. We said a fresh start that will be explained to you later. We can't show you before all is ready. The only thing we want you to do is trust, relax and enjoy your day. I never really died then and never will. Forever an eternal living CHRIST.

Love and light with laughter. TttA

EASY DOES IT!

When you relax all conditions will improve and it takes will go smooth. Start each task by taking a deep breath and ask for assistance. Cooperation is also important. Sorting and sifting takes time but you will benefit later when you keep all in order. To be practical will also combine with ease therefore everything will operate much better. Today's event went better when you asked us to prepare the grounds. Your buffer zone has improved so you can do what's needed in a shorter time and enjoy part of it. Later on it will get better still. That will also keep your faith and trust in us. It's been a long time coming and plenty of obstacles under the travels. Don't mix up or take short cuts the pattern is important for you so you can feel more comfortable. It's all a learning time when it's called for. Start a fresh after a relaxing day.

Lots of love, laughter and leisure. TttA

TRY AND TRY AGAIN!

Watch out for the pattern that is trying to deter you or make you late. Learn from the pattern of life. Lately you have seen more than usual of pattern forming. The alert signals are very clear. Take note and just wait. When situations arise that is to show you interference and disruptions. The same again tell us, and then wait for the solutions. If nothing happens put on standby mode. We still are holding on to the reins. A big battle is going on in the universe. Do not despair it will be O.K. but in our time not Earth time. In the waiting time do something practical and enjoy life as it comes. Last night was to annoy you and take your energy. It did not work and they have to pay a big price for making mistakes. Well we are now dealing with it. Leave that lot to us. It is the fastest solution and the best. Have a great day and enjoy what comes your way.

Blessings and wisdom.TttA

TOGETHER AGAIN!

Some days you are so busy so the order of the day is to set time apart and let no one or nothing more important take place of our time together. So much is being dealt with and so many are trying to disrupt and your work for the light. You are aware of greed, jealousy and envy. Especially from women they should realise that the price is to answer for all happenings. Many are already controlled by negative forces so they are told to do so. Danger and no growth will follow, then what ever they do until a change has taken place for a direction to the light. We are asking all light workers to stay firm, positive and wise for times to come. Support each other and do take time out when called for. You will know by the way they speak and act towards you. The exposure is obvious to you but many would not observe and understand the picture given and the energy around them is revealing.

Love and light TttA

HOLD ON!

When pressures appear, stop and ask for help. Humans are not at all times able to see what's going on before making a statement. Let us deal with it and stand back. Forces are at work beyond your experience. As you go along you will see when to start and when to stop. At present time you are experiencing so many adverse conditions so stay alert, calm and ask us what to do and how much. When tired rest and drink plenty of water, stay clear of sweet food. It will ease up but because of the universal war you are picking other dimensions unease. Rest after all work done today and tomorrow you will awaken as new. We are still guarding you so leave all conditions to us. We have helped you to find most of the things that were misplaced or aborted. The rest will come to light later. Calm will once again rein. Keep on working one day at a time. It will be sorted. We are putting extra light around you and your work, plus all positive connections.

Thank you. TttA

KEEP UP THE GOOD WORK!

It's a blessing when you keep going and found a joy by carry on doing so. My energy and light will refill you and strengthen you. Life has taken a different turn than what you expected so learn from it and be grateful that someone is looking after your interest. You ask for proof and you got it. Don't look back on old mistakes or decisions made in honesty and trust. Still we say listen in and spread the good news to all that's prepared and willing to learn and accept. The wisdom is at times strewn on stony ground so stop doing so. We prepare the soil so let us do that. Envy greed and plain level of not hearing or being controlled is often of be littering you and your work for the light. They should look at their own lives and stop and stop interfering without being asked. Still respect others opinion but it's up to you if you believe it or not. At least you will know where they are on their spirit journey. If genuine it will show up if not it will fail. Stay close.

Loving thoughts. TttA

ORDER!

Let order help and enhance you. It will save you a lot of time and energy. You are doing just that. The last few days you have sorted and order in many areas. When busy it's very easy to mislay some objects and keep in mind the same goes for your spirit life. Don't get too busy with life so you forget the daily order of your work for spirit. That is still not an order from us only a request to aid you for your work. To get a better clearer picture what's going on. Life is busy and you should try not to get pulled in to it, you are not here for that kind of life. You have lived so many hundreds of lifetimes so all that are experienced before. This time is to learn and go higher. With all that needed for your growth. Still help others and tell them you know it feels like. Sadness will turn in to joy. Keep on seeing life how it is and why. Acceptance it's the only way when you can't change it.

Courage and wisdom! TttA

JOY WILL COME!

Believe that is so and it will come. To prepare and think ahead is not always possible but you can work on more joyful thoughts. Yesterday you did ask for signs and you got them. Ask more and claim more. We still will only give it if it's right for you and your development. It's all again back to the divine law and cause and effect. Many think in today's world. You can get away with that not so you don't have to cheat with it. Hand it over to us Faster and more accurate and no karma will come back on you. Think of life like a school of life. You have told that so many times. And that still stands. Different levels for so many but you can't compare. It's your journey. No one should take another's lessons on. That will not aid anyone. The revelation you had is to show you how many would like to deter you. Keep on going as you are.

Blessings and love. TttA

GIVE OF THE ETERNAL
LIGHT AND LOVE

As you get some from us give out half and keep the other half for yourself. Always give out of your knowledge, love and healing. Otherwise you will not be a good vessel to use for the light. If stagnation occurs you must look at your taking and giving. It must be an exchange. If not, one will be depleted and you will need to rest. The balance of it all to get you to understand the universal and spiritual laws. These laws are forever and nothing is altering; only people do. It's O.K. when moving upwards not follow the crowds of life. Like a flock of sheep without a shepherd. Look back to the old times and you will remember about sheep and lost ones. You will have your part in the work when we think you are able and willing. Forget the self and get ready to go to the frontline once again. We will give you the strength and wisdom to handle it all. Still we say carry out what is on your plate.

Love. TttA

STAY FOCUSED!

It is most important to do so, because otherwise you could easily get side tracked or lose your time where you need to see the pattern. When you discover what is in the picture it will help you to nail down what to do, for the next step. Many still are trying to wear the mask but that does not work anymore. It's better for you to stay clear of that kind of treatment. When you feel like moving around do so. Later on you will go further but for now stay calm and clear. Others should know better than stealing from you, or don't show any respect. It's a waste that lesson is now learned. You have other situations to deal with. Your special nights are indeed very special. Many get help, healing and meet holy spirits. This is for you to know and accept. Whoever is coming is sent by us, so welcome them in the name of the light. Keep working as you are and you will see the rewards coming. Only genuine searching souls will benefit.

Courage my friend. TttA

REJOICE!

Be glad and rejoice that you are still working, growing and experiencing healing wisdom and protection. Many people stoop down to feel greed envy and jealousy. It'd be a waste of time and will show up your level of understanding and growth. The exposing is just a sign of low level of development. Well now once again you are being told about life and its movements. Your own movement will strengthen and keep you flexible. This time of the year you are more pruned to sit for too long so keep in mind to move more once every hour. As the weather changes remember to go outside and watch the season changing in to all the colours of nature and how the animals react. The nature is very close to you and the strong life force that goes with it. Today will show up as a revealing day. News from afar and locally. Keep on going as you are. The work that you are asked to do is of future value. Don't ask only follow through.

Courage and love from us all. TttA

ANOTHER SEASON-ANOTHER REASON!

Be vigilant and listen in as the season is changing once again. The reason is for all to stop and recharge, and rest in all areas. The growth will come with a fresh outlook. The pruning is all necessary to give all a better chance for undergrowth. All lives are individual so treat them as such. Every person that comes across you and the work you are doing is there for a reason. If and when they go is for a further growth. Else were or the seed has fallen on stony ground. It's not up to you it never was. The only thing is to accept what we bring you to learn from. Life is so different for you –but it is for a reason. Too much time on your Earth dimension would take too much of energy and time. See it for what it is. Your NI friend down south is starting to pack up and soon moving for next stop and work. You will hear so stay patient. Enjoy today and gather your thoughts. Your conditions is being healed by us. We know that you know.

Blessings and love from us all. TttA

ANOTHER DAY- ANOTHER CHANCE!

Let that be a lesson to remember. A new day- a fresh start. Don't think too much what about what did or did not happen yesterday. It's all a test and today you will get another. All went well we were with you all the way thanks for the trust in us as it is still working. Today's warm weather will also help to make you feel better. Let us give you the inspiration and wisdom to carry out your work. Don't make it to be a chore. Gladly do what's on the agenda. Don't give up only wait a little while when you come across adversity. As your field is getting stronger you will venture further out. The life giving force is there so claim it. All in good time and you will enjoy it to the full, when you get your confirmation and spend less time trying to understand.

Some subjects are above your education. Keep on asking for more and we will give it to you gradually. If nothing comes through wait for clearance. Keep occupied and rest in between. We have your concern in our hands.

Thank you for working. TttA

STICK TO YOUR GOALS!

Let us encourage and support you in your quest for growth. It takes plenty of discipline and plenty of strength with focus. Let that be your words for today. You are growing and advancing. It has taken a lot of time but that will not matter. Now when you have sorted so many situations out you will have more time for your work and time out to do nothing. It's understandable when you look back to see what went on but it had to be done to show you. Well now let your day unfold as much as possible and enjoy what is coming your way. Yesterday you did try something new to see it could be done after all. That was very beneficial for you. Today is another version of an old situation, it will turn out just fine. Trust and faith is very much of value. Don't concern yourself over others woes, leave all to us. You are doing better in that area. Go ahead with next plan and do remember exercise and water, It's necessary for your rejuvenation.

Blessings and care .TttA

ALL IN GOOD TIME!

If and when you feel like moving, wait and check. It all will happen when it is supposed to. When all conditions are right for all involved in, activates the energy and all will come to pass. Leave all the activations to us and you only have to claim and we will hear you. Only remember what's good for your higher self will benefit your growth. We are still your guides and healers No one can have a better teacher than us. Stay patient and listen in and do what's required of you. Again and again you have been tried and checked. The work you are being assigned is for all mankind. Stand by and accept your part as a service to the spiritual realm. Tonight you will have the presence of us again. Stranger each time until you see. You have been waiting for such a long time that is proof that you are patient. Days when nothing shows up are still fruitful, so carry on with your work. Freedom to live is very helpful at all times. Smile and enjoy what comes your way.

Cheers and light. TttA

BLESSED BE!

So much in such a short time, you really have seen the dark side having a field day. Well they did not daunt or discourage you. You are stronger and stronger as a result. So they really have done you a favour by alerting you to their dirty tactics. The last days of the month have to be the last days of interruptions and other blockages. You have done your part and more most times. Enjoy the harmony and balance that will come at once. Try to stop other activities when the events come at once. We were with you today all day and you did quite well after all after all that mixture. Value the true blue people. The stress just has to stay outside. Some don't realise what they have been doing to be led by the wrong master is not causing any growth only decay. Today's work is coming out for the best Universal disturbance is now clear. Yesterday it was a moon eclipse that confused very many. That is gone so tomorrow is a brand new day. Go slow and enjoy what comes. Thank you for standing by.

Eternally yours. TttA

GIVE WARMTH AND LOVE!

That is what we want you to do today. You don't have to see or physically meet them. Your thoughts are getting a wide range of power love and wisdom out to whomever you feel needs it. You are picking up their needs and wants so meet them in true spirit. You are getting better at receiving us and you will see. The withdrawal time is not a waste. It's really work being done. We know that you are trying very hard to understand what who and when. Let it all unfold in its own good time. You know deep down what's going on but you would like proof because of all lies in the past from so called psychic's and non-spiritual entities. We do know how isolated you feel. That's part of your training to be able to hear us better. Other times will come but we are making sure that you know the whole picture. Hidden agendas are also hard at times. Bear with it and then detach from every case. Teach others to cut and detach from all angles.

Love and wisdom. TttA

CUT AND DETACH!

Once again you have been tested about just that subject. You did better than last time. Say stop and don't let anyone take your time. Listen but don't get involved. We have explained that to you so many times. I will have more practise later in the week. Today you have had another revelation. You were surprised but not shocked. Other tools will be given to you and what has been taken is of no value whatsoever for anyone else. They might have thought so but the information is not complete for anyone else. Except you. Stop clear and take heart that you found out now. All will be sorted in the time we give you. Many people will try to find out about you that you don't know and they are trying to find faults. That's no good that is only showing you were they are and it is no good to come back to you. Very many others needs and wants will be met. Let the rest of the day unfold smoothly. We are looking in to the whole situation and remember how to cut off. The ladies are not too happy now but that's not your problem.

Blessings and love. TttA

FOCUS!

Keep on practising just that. Nothing will completely be accomplished when you are not concentrating enough. Many times you are doing your best but at present condition is going on. So all you can do is keeping on practising. We do understand where you are. It's been a revealing week so far, and more to come. To expose a situation is to understand. Why so many are getting lessons about their actions towards themselves and others. Today you were given proof and again we say. Study in detail what's going on. It's not always the obvious that you need to look at as most are hiding behind two or three masks, according to their beliefs or who is in charge. Well now it's clear how so many perceive you. Still we say leave all of that to us. The ones that come back are willing to learn and you don't have to ask us. You will know. Your new group is forming again. It will be more respectful.

Eternal love and light. TttA

FEEL THE WARMTH FROM MY SON AND THE SUN!

Try your best to soak up the rays from the sun and welcome the love from my son. As the days grow shorter the need to use the rays are very important. It will help you in days to come. Enjoy being able to sit in the sun and enjoy all that energy coming in to your body. We do know how much it will help you and give you strength to be able to carry out your tasks. Every light worker has their assignment, so do only yours. The training testing is severe but necessary. We are making sure that you fully understand what is yours to deal with. We will give special attention for tomorrow. More souls are ready to come and experience other spheres. When you work and rest in peace you will achieve much more. That was proven today again. Keep on trying and trusting you are getting better and stronger. Remind others also about the living water and drink plenty of it. Bless it and feel the benefit as you do. Sit by the well and rest for a while. The water will as well as the wisdom while I wait there with you.

Blessings from heaven. TttA

SOLDIER ON!

As well as you can. Don't overdo any subject or push yourself to hard. You are still inclined to do so at times. Like we often have said do your best and we will do the rest. There is a right time for action and a time for rest you have to do is carry out what you have been given to deal with. It will get better and we are always there for you. Today you could see what the story was for you to learn from. Still listen and completely detach. The cut of point is different for each soul.so ask us. The individual is still of much value. The technical situation is all back to balance again. It's hard to know art times, you wish to have a better picture but the planetary system is influencing so much. All technical situations are getting sorted. Tonight is a healing time and also explanations will be given to the ones that asked. Rest until you feel the calm from within has taken place.

Cheer and joy. TttA

USE THE SUNLIGHT!

That is a very valuable way to get your metals, plants, animals and humans clean clear and restarted. I am sending healing warmth and joy with the rays of light. The most natural source of energy and growth. Many would as usual disagree, so let them. You know better than to question me. Many times you have not fully understood what we have meant, but you are getting there. Last night's meeting went well with all tuning in and receiving news. We will send you more genuine souls to enter and have a chance to understand. The others will not do you any more harm.

Your own protection is stronger now. So go ahead unafraid and brave. Let today go in harmony and joy. Count your blessings and enjoy what comes for your benefit. Keep on being positive and the music will do the rest. Still keep up the discipline as much as possible. The pendulums are now clean so you can ask us which one is best. You also have asked to get clearer answers that you can trust. We will check that for you too. More tomorrow.

Blessings TttA

LISTEN TO NATURE!

Take notice of the sounds of nature. It might be the wind waves or birds. The natural ways are the best of all. If it's not feeling natural or feels uncomfortable, then leave it alone. Many situations could have been avoided for so many if they had followed their gut feelings. It's a big lesson for some and a very natural way for others. That part is nothing to do with you. Only be an observer of life. Stay back if not any questions have been asked. Beware of too much talk. Some are just lonely so they want connections and feedback. That is life all over again. People will be people. Still we say don't alter anything if not told. Your unease at times comes from your surroundings. Build a stronger buffer zone. Detach from situations that's positive for now. Keep on with your other occupational work. It is not enough balance in one area, so it's making waves in others that we will help you with. All is indeed in good working condition, and it is coming together at last.

Courage and love for all. TttA

LET LIFE FLOW!

When you think about it stagnation is not good for anyone. Stop and rest when needed, but don't let your life. Spirit, mind, body and emotions stagnate. Ask what to do and follow up checking. Maintain what you can and don't overdo it. It could become an obsession. You have seen so many with just that situation. The same goes for your spirit growth. When out of inspirations go to nature. Change your outlook and enjoy what you have. Appreciate others good will and get your joy from be able to see and do as much as you can .Compere with anyone else does not come in to it. Its human but it is not of any spiritual value. We are still there for you and whoever asks in honesty. But we can't get help without being asked. The same if anyone else needs your help they have to ask. Only then you can pass it on to us. Today will give you what you want so you can pass on to others from your overflow. That will mean no stagnation. Remember the lake, no inflow no out flow. It will shrink after a while and dry up.

Courage and love. TttA

SUNNY GREETINGS!

Enjoy the sun and watch how the gardens grow. Even animals and all living things will benefit from the rays of the rays of the living sun. Peace and harmony is to come to your planet once more after the war. Some have been overcome. Stay clear of uneasy people and situations that are not for your benefit. Thus people stand out more and make you see who is not threatening you. According to whom you are, not what they want you to be. The subtle ness of them is very obvious. You have seen their ways or many have listened to others that could be very convincing. The subtleness of some is also very obvious. You have seen their ways so once again be an observer and learn from it. No one should throw pearls to swine. It's their loss and now it's too late. You did more than your share. Walk tall and look up, you don't ever have to feel that way again. Enough is enough. Well rest and relax for the rest of the day. The strain after last week's needs to go away. All is well and say it very often.

Healing wisdom and grace. TttA

PEACE IN THE STORM!

Calm and peace is the cure for most illnesses. To be able to stay calm in the warzone is a big test. It will work and it is a good destroyer of all negativity. Keep that in mind when you are dealing with life and all the situations that have arrived of late. Many think about life in monetary values that's human but that is not showing any priorities of what's most important for your spiritual growth. Everybody wants the basics of life but to reach for things that are not needed is only greed and that's not good for the soul. If any lack appears in some arias ask us and we will supply it for you. The world would appear a different place if all that deceit, greed and envy was taken away. All you all can do is sending love and light to the planet and all living thing on it. Your detachment skills are improving. You have of areas that you can practise on. We still keep an eye on your life and how you handle situations. Yesterday you did have more proof of healing. All is in working order.

Eternal blessings and strength. TttA

LET IT ALL FLOW!

Back to NO stagnation, only have a rest when you are tired. So much more is coming through when you are relaxed and undisturbed. Keep the silence at all costs. We speak to you in our language we know that you will understand. Many would not think it's right or perhaps it's not time. Too many suspicious minds and the antichrist is about. You already know that so they will show up clearer to you now than before. To have a clear outlook is of most value for your work. We will help you to get your lost items returned. It's a part of your tools so no one can use them against you.

One fine day they will give up and go to try and annoy somebody else. Detach from all this situations. You have others to attend to and you will. Let today be a day of light, love and wisdom. We will connect you further with other powerful teachers. You will feel when and where. Many rich blessings for you and your work for the light.

Amen to that. TttA

USE THE COLOURS!

This time of the year to enhance your lives, you only needed a reminder from old times so you know its working others new to the idea can start with the colour chart and practise every day. Yesterday you experienced more honesty and a lot more feedback. The little interruptions did not come to very much. Stupid entities trying to daunt you it worked the opposite way .We will make sure they will get the message. You are becoming a mighty force for the light, so you will be given more tools and responsibilities. Still we say a day at a time will get you there. No one is stronger than us your teacher, healers and guides. You know that is so and reinforcement is always good. Tonight will also be strong and encouraging. Let it all unfold and we will do the rest. Let others come to you we have spoken to their spirit to do so. It's all a big plan for us to deal with so do your part and all will be well.

Blessings and love. TttA

LET THERE BE LIGHT!

Spread my light to the needy and sad world. Many would not know where it is coming from but they will feel it. Like a lightning for some. They will see a rainbow of light or a strong light ray of glorious light through the clouds. It does not matter how you see the only way that's right for you. People are so finely tuned in so they only need a little sign, others want a higher light to reach through. Well now we meet again last night all that was meant to be the way it was. Healing was given to both of you in full and more throughout the night. To know is not enough to be wise is a lot better. This morning you had proof that all will be well in its all good time. The main thing is to leave it all to us to hold the reins. The pink colour is still with you and is staying. Enjoy and keep as you are. Your life is unfolding where it is beneficial for you and your work.

Blessings and love. TttA

THE SUN WILL BREAK THROUGH!

Go out and let someone know that a solution is coming. Never give up only let go to get a better grip. Time is still of the essence so use it wisely. You have seen a lot of that lately to support the idea we have given you in so many different versions. We are still very much behind your work as you will grow when you have more freedom to teach and advise. Some are still trying very hard to interrupt, but to no avail anymore. You are doing all you can to aid detach and advance. As we have said so many times before it takes focus and discipline to work as you do. The ones that do not know feel envy are not very well informed. They only see what they think and what appears to be to them. Leave all of that once again. We do know how hard you work at detachment and its working very well. Today will show you that again. A little surprise is in store for you as an encouragement.

Eternal blessings. TttA

THE CLOUDS WILL GO!

For ever-you do know that the clouds will go it's only temporary to be able to show you the actions of people and situations. Watch nature and follow the tide. You are beginning to see that is so. Everything has its season, so don't concern yourself events do not appear or get changed. That how it should be. When it is waiting time, wait. Life has many lessons to teach you all about cause and effect. Every belief and creed on your planet is really the same truth in different versions, so it does not change anything it's only a different version to get to the goal, and is of different appearance. The third dimension has so many illusions. It fools many but not you. Long ago you nearly fell for it-but in the last minute you walked away. It is a big test to see how you react and how calm you will be. Back to the tall trees in the storm. You have seen them bending-but never break. Let that be many peoples lesson.

Blessings for your next 24 hours. TttA

MAINTENANCE!

Keep an eye on how much care you want to give away and how much energy to maintain life, for yourself and others. To be able to exchange care, wants and upliftment for each day. You have seen what that has been done if not followed. It becomes a state of numbness and stagnation if allowed to carry on. It will be hard to untangle and heal up. In your line of work you have come across so many that have left situations go on for 30 years or more. Still it's never too late to start afresh and look at life with new eyes and ears. The courses of these situations are many and some very complex. It's a tangled web we weave at times. It's normally coming on for years and at the end no one knows any different and just carry on. Every ones situation is so personal so it would need a personal treatment. Let today unfold as best as you can. Keep warm and relax with music.

Blessings and warm love. TttA

LIGHT AND LOVE

Remember to use these two words most of the day. This time of the year many need more input of our love and light. Frozen souls and sad hearts is the ground for depression and anger you all have more of these lessons around you and inside you in one life time or the other. Let go of when it was happening and ask us to clear the thoughts-no longer valid now. Today you will get a wonderful surprise that is a sign to encourage you to carry on your work. A plateau is fine when waiting for more input or take a little rest to see the overview of life itself. Think of an eagle how they fly and see the bird's eye view. When down you can't expect to see clearly what's going on so look up, go up and stand up. A different outlook is all it takes to renew your strength. Keep warm from the inside and let it spread out to all that comes onto your path. The Christ in me salutes the Christ in you. Think about the recognition in that truth.

Warmest blessings. TttA

USE THE RAYS FROM THE SUN!

The sun is always there even if of late that has not been seen. The inner life needed to be worked at so you and many others to look deeper into the life force, and enjoy the recharging. We have ways to let you know about all the different faces of development. Different for some but souls are so individual so in most needs to follow. Tonight you will experience a change in some. We are doing our work and you yours. It's all a combined effort to get all work done. Most of our light workers are specialized so your training is also the same. It has taken years of study and focusing to be able to empty out and receive more truth. Have one more look at priorities and boundaries-you do but a little reminder to recall our teachings. Your book rather ours is coming out exactly the right time and effort from us. And the three of you. Remember today is today, take care of it.

Eternal blessings TttA

ETERNAL BLESSINGS!

Let us give you a gift of blessings. So much more is coming your way when you let us come in to your life. Don't for a moment think that you can do all by yourself. Certain tasks can be done and a really good result when you do operate. Many links make a strong chain and when one link is getting worn or broken, look at once for any breakage or other blockage. Replace or restore so it is all in good working condition. Well now another connection was activated last night. Trust us to send the right souls to you. You will also have more practise and feel the power coming through. More will be sent, similar but with other needs. That does not matter only for you to do your work as promised before you were born. Your spirit is very strong and in charge, as is should have been always. Your garden is very useful for many reasons that you know that to be so. We have borrowed some of your tools until august for your benefit and later for others. Keep up your discipline and courage.

Always your loving teachers. TttA

GO AHEAD!

Leave the planning to us and then we will give your part to carry out. We know very well how capable you are to do more then you are doing. Training times are here to keep on working as you are. We are aware of your quests and so many questions. Your curious nature is helpful many times. Today you got another request. We do endorse that by our angel David to do what we said. The following through is very important. You of all people are very aware of the law of the universe. The new contact for spirit will be very useful and help you to advance in your work. Today you will hear more news and some will come and talk. Your home is ours to use so we will come so we will speak to thus who needs to come to get help one way or the other. Your commitment is great so keep on trusting and learning. We will speak to the ones that need to communicate and make sure they get the message.

Keep writing and learning. TttA

ONE DAY AT A TIME!

Spread your work energy and subjects throughout your day. Too much of anything is not good for anyone or anything. Back to balance in your life. In all four areas you would like more balance. As you are so sensitive to feelings of others you pick up so much and have now learned to get rid of all negative feelings, except when tired and exhausted. Thus times you need to watch for wrong decisions. These could easily be made so look at your energy level before making a decision. Never rush in to anything as it's only there to test you and see if you have learned from our teaching. Don't give too much sympathy stay professional and all will be well. Treat yourself and others with detachment to stop getting emotional. We still are watching over you and your work. So keep on spreading light and love to the world. Don't be used let them do their own homework only get them started. Lately you have so much on your plate as you could handle and you have.

Best wishes. TttA

SPREAD THE LIGHT!

Yes my children of light do just that, also light a light. It all will help to lighten up your thoughts and spirit. This time of the year you need extra input from us to be able to keep up with your love and light output to all. Let no one or no incident block your channel to us. We know that very many are trying to block you that will work in your favour because you work harder to keep on track. Still it's testing times so stay close to the shore. Many want to come but conditions block the way. All of that will go in time so leave that entire situation to us. The usage you are making at night is benefitting all and strengthen the ropes between us. The light that you are bringing back is also healing for yourself and all that comes in contact with you. Today is a new day so treat it as such. The tools that you are missing are indeed great tools. We have borrowed them for a very good purpose. They will be returned when the work is done.

Blessings and light. TttA

S.O.S.-SAVE OUR SOULS!

How important that is a life nothing else is. That is a very old saying easy to remember. As of old which I spoke in parables the same is often used today. Nothing else is really of much value. First look at the level of energy that goes and comes from the soul of a person than you can tell what's going on at the moment. Also because of the solution is very personal for each individual it helps to know the cause of the disturbances. Many have an outside or alien so the wide interest from so many directions could cause an uneasy feeling. The solution is to ask for all that to cleared and have a clear channel to be able to receive more of our truth. To be able to do that will benefit you and the ones that ask for your help. It's all a big strong connection and most beneficial for all of you. Today will prove to be a very interesting in one more way. Keep up your work and we are all behind you.

Eternal blessings TttA

WE BLESS YOUR NEW DAY!

We always do but you at times are too busy to notice. Your trust in us was shown again yesterday. The lady in question was so weary and exhausted so their input was very beneficial, for her and also for you to see her change. At times you ask what for today. Well now that is not for you to decide, it's our input and work, together with you to enhance the universal spirit work. You do your part and leave others to theirs. Many will come back to you and want to learn more. Some felt that they don't understand you, but their spirit did, but was not in charge so the critical side came out and it did hit you. Ask us to smooth the way in your kind of work. It needs to be a cooperation, and coordination to be able to work fully. Today will also proof to be very interesting. You will be surprised when the day is over. How much has been done. Blessings and lots of love.

Congratulations to your friend A.A

Keep your work going we are behind you. TttA

LET US AID YOUR LIFE!

Open up and empty out so that you can receive what we are bringing you help to support and guide you throughout the day. So much gets lost when not emptied out, so it's full everywhere spirit mind and body with emotions. Keep sharing what goodness you have, but the inlet must be clear and free. Go ahead and check once again. Input was given to help you carry through your tasks. We are forever guiding you because some do not understand your work so they are trying to ruin your work or what you do or say. All that is really happening is that they are hitting us. Well that's not acceptable still we say act on our requests and don't get put off by small interruptions. Tonight will prove to be very interesting and joyful. The numbers will not make any difference to us.

Blessings and love. TttA

GREETINGS!

Let today be a great day and speak to the once that are ready to listen. Others will not be making an attempt to understand what's going on. The same people live for the day, others will look for a more permanent solution. To live and how to best do your learning and grow from it. No stagnation in my kingdom only rest and regroup. The diamond of the truth is there and you know that to be so. The further you go you can see how tangled and unnecessary webs have been grown. Peel off the outer layer of disguise and look at the core. The truth is quite often hidden if not the person is ready to see. So look at the picture as you evolve you can see clearer what there is to see. The pearl is hidden in a shell until its ready to open. The same goes for people. When they are ready to come out and shine you will see why the events took so long time to come to anything valuable. Today you will uncover so many more facts.

And then you will make the situations so much clearer.

Eternal blessings. TttA

LET MY SUN SHINE!

Go out and feel the love from all living things. The nature forces are so life giving and good to connect with. Use nature as a healer and helper. Last week's incident could have been avoided if alertness was more at the core. You are most of the times but still increase a little more of your awareness. No one has to be perfect and work towards the goal. Today you will get another chance to see some sides of your visitors that you have not seen before. We are aware of the ones that are trying to disturb you and your group. All of that is in your hands, we are dealing and informing them. The message will get through, your work will increase and you will have victory. You know which way you mean. The love and concern you have for other souls is fine, but detach from sympathy and feeling.

Sorry, that has never ever helped anyone. You have known that for some years and you are following through. Have confidence that all is working for your benefit. Stay tuned.

Joy, love and wisdom. TttA

SURRENDER!

Surrender to the source of love and light. You do so and tell others if they want progress and growth. At times you have much work and other times none. One day it will be in balance, your whole life will be so much better and you will perform miracles in our name. The working time will be spent in further work and development. Today is different again. You never know these days who is coming or who is going. That's applies for all conditions in conciseness. As you are picking so much from others you need to explain very firmly what's on your mind. Time alone outside will give you some of the answers. We are doing our best to inform you through the best way as a password. Don't get stressed in any situation. Ever again surrender and ask us to deal with it. Some situations are very involved. So don't try to work them out. Many try to blame others for mistakes made and no one should. All men are free to decide for themselves. People will be people and you are not responsible for others deeds and actions, and so is everyone for all thoughts and actions for every day.

Amen to that. TttA

PEACE AND HARMONY
WILL REIGN AGAIN!

Let no one put asunder what we have built together. Many would like to destroy but the only thing that they destroy is themselves. Don't let one day go before you have done the best what you can and have your priorities in good order. Every day you have opportunities to deal with. Learn how to look at life with our eyes and thoughts. Be outside when you can and enjoy hours of calmness and get a refill from nature. All the little things that are going on is to learn about oppositions. Deal with it and don't give it any energy. Certain people are in lack of just that. Everybody needs to look at how much to give away and how much to keep for themselves. Many are struggling to get on top of the situations that have accumulated throughout many years. It would be wise to let it go once and for all. Back to forgive, forget and then realise it. If not all time has been dealt with it is not clear only buried. Guard your spirit so no more incidents will occur to be dealt with later.

Go ahead on your path with blessings. TttA

BLESSED BE THIS DAY!

Yes my children of light, I make all things new. When the time is right it just will happen. Some people are playing games with you make belief or silly words. You are aware what's going on. Little do they know how much you really know and who you are connected to. Today is a new day so do what's needed and enjoy all the new input we are giving you. That is also including the connections that are around you and respecting you and your work. The others are not aware enough to be able to understand as yet. Carry out your part of the eternal work and leave others to theirs. Your other 4 books will be understood after the shift. It's all connected so it will move when all parts are coming together and working like one force. United you will conquer and keep on giving support to like-minded souls. When you raise above it all and look from above the picture will clear and you can see much better. Stand back and be an observer. Most times it will save a lot of unnecessary situations to arise.

Blessed be. TttA

ALL IN GOOD TIME!

The solution is there but not all ingredients are ready. Wait and develop a lot of patience. As your work goes along you will be faster, do spot unease and discord anywhere. The solution to all these cases we will give you as you ask. Trust is a big part of your lesson, so ask for more and it will be given in an instant. Ours is the time to know when and how. Today you will experience another milestone. It's all as it should be, you are puzzled at times, because of so many happenings but that's a reactivating of energies. Going on a little longer and you really will see wonders unfold. Use the heat today to freshen up what's needed. Tonight will be another lesson learned. You will know straight away what we are talking about. Go along your path and keep the good work up. You are learning every day about spirit and people. Your physical is getting sorted so follow through. Work and rest in equal proportion is best for you.

Eternal joy and blessing. TttA

TRUST AND OBEDIENCE!

Let the trust in us and some humans increase. It's very hard for you at times. Too much is happening to trying to put you off your course. One day it will not be a daunting task for you. Lighter and brighter times will come. Many are running a race nearly to the very end and when the goal is in site they give up. Watch for that situation. On Tuesday it will be another shift for Mother Earth. It's all happening according to plan. Follow through and when nothing is happening wait and let us sort out what is next. The different speed for different souls is apparent, but that is not of great value. Only what is being worked at under the journey. You all still are coming across adversity-not for much longer the test for you is to accept what cannot be changed, and also see the good things that come your way. Remember to see it as a lesson and not take is an interruption. Bless this new day and let it all unfold as it may. The future experiences are still hidden for you .Only a little at the time, will be revealed, for your own benefit. Some come and some go is an experience through space and time.

All our wisdom. TttA

EMPTY OUT AND LISTEN IN!

This time when you are in need of wisdom, strength and joy you would be wise to follow our guidance. The more complicated the task is the more time to withdraw and listen to us. The supply will be there and don't concern yourself with how much or when. Deal with not more than two situations at once, you don't have to go on so many different levels of knowledge at the same time. As we have said so many times you cannot give the same treatment to everyone because people are individuals and should be treated as such. Tender loving care and listen in silence until you get the O K from us. As from old you were a confessional for so many. It helps when you know a person is listening and understanding. Lately quite a few have found their way to you and we did send them to you as we said we would. Your personal life is about to alter for the better. So trust laugh and relax. Are guarding you day and night.

Blessings for all. TttA

BE STILL AND KNOW THAT I AM GOD!

To be able to be still in today's conditions are indeed a gift. We do understand and are sending extra help for all unexpected incidents. Stay very close to the source and enjoy getting the energy and love. The source always supplies all your needs. Some get tools of value other gets food, spirit mental and physical. All four areas are taken care of. No one can treat one side and don't expect the other to be the same. It's all to do with life force and input from us. The main thing is that you must ask for and don't act before you ask us, so we can activate the supplies. Go on today with your maintenance and relax with the tools we have given you. Others will try to distract and daunt you that will not work anymore. It has been a very trying time for you and many light workers. All have been tested and tried in many ways. Let that be a lesson for you all. To stay firm loving and joyful under thus circumstances is also very tiring. Keep on going and don't lose sight of your goals.

Love light and upliftment. TttA

JOIN TOGETHER!

United we stand, divided you will fall. This time you are advised to stay very close to the source, and do your best to stay positive. Tomorrow will tell a story about Earth and its inhabitants. The halftime shift is another sign of the planning of the big blueprint of Earth. Certain events cannot be altered; it's all in the universal plan. Most prophets throughout the centuries were told so much important news most of them have lived before their time, so they were misunderstood and often killed for their beliefs. Society is made that way so many don't look who they are following. Habits are fine as long as they are good and reliable. Many have just got carried away and taken by the wayside. Always stop if uneasy to look at your journey, where is it taking you and who are your companions. The weekend was silent but good work was done and once again you past the test. Carry out todays work in an orderly manner. We are still there and guarding you.

Your loving team. TttA

ENJOY THE LIFE-GIVING
RAYS OF MY SUN!

Take care of all warmth and energy from the universal storehouse. It's full of supplies for every need and want. If only more would realise how easy it is to get refilled and then work so much easier and more joyful for us, especially today when the two planets are meeting. The big picture is affected more than the earth inhabitants know. That is not for you to deal with only observe. Trust and faith is still a big part of all that are evolving. Many cases that you have met are so uneasy about trust and faith so trust something that they don't see is hard for them. By giving practical examples you will show many how it's been for you many times. Most people will only listen when somebody else has gone through something similar to themselves. That is a good way so keep on using that as a tool. Relay most of what we give you as it is just that. It might seem like something else to others but that is not your concern. Most have a task or lesson to deal with each lifetime so they should get on with it.

All our love, support and blessings. TttA

STAY CLOSE AND REFILL!

Let's work together and enjoy the union. We do every day but at times you have too many subjects going, so time is very important. This time of the year you are colder and the sun lower. The time spent in work is more energy taking. Today when working with spirit you were attacked again. The force was strong but once again you manage to deal with it. Your system is so finely tuned in so you feel everything much stronger. You have to ask for a stronger guard so you can operate better for yourself and for us. You know what's happening before it does and that's why you feel so weary at times. Bear with it and ask for daily strength from us. Trust in the source and leave us to do our work. Many cases are for you only to request our input to deal with so many different levels of understanding.

You are working as hard as you are able, so unwinding is called for. Priorities are also on the agenda. The balance is out again because of the alterations in the universe. Let us uplift and gladden you.

Courage and love. TttA

STAY POSITIVE AND CALM!

Never for a moment give in to thinking that is sad, bad or negative. Always look at the bright sunny side. Today is a day of inside work, so reflect on your lighthouse as it is doing great work for human kind. It's a very powerful tool for us. We lead you to it so you can see how well everything is organised. The work that needed to be activated is now happening. So much unexpected is going on everywhere. Books and studying is fine as long as you don't get carried away with all different ideas, and forget to first go to the source of all knowledge. You are seeing so many situations unfold so watch and observe. Take care of your soul first and all other situations will follow. Keep warm and joyful and take the day that unfolds in the best way as possible. We are still guarding and informing you about work rest and time out, as we have said so many times before. Follow through as best as you can and we will do the rest. The cleaning is being worked on. Cheers from all of us.

A sparkle is turning in to a flame. TttA

KEEP ON PROGRESSING!

Many times you have been thinking that you have not progressed fast enough. That's only a negative thought or to put it more plainly it is that you are too closed to yourself. It's hard to see yourself and what's happening. Be an observer and stand back then you will see a wider picture. Today will be another catch up day. Get ready for the new you and enjoy the little things that come your way. Don't ever take people for granted. Their actions speak for themselves and you will know by what feelings you pick up and what their eyes are telling you. Your intuition is very strong so go with that. Some changes in your environment will occur for the better for you and whoever is visiting. We still are making sure whoever is entering will feel safe and calm. Keep on doing your routine that will enhance your life. And we still are doing the rest for you. The situation that you are dealing with is all in hand. The universal picture is in remaking.

Blessings and love. TttA

KEEP GOING IN TRUST!

It's all about surrender and trust. Once again you have had proof of just that. It has taken a long time to check and double check. The time facts it's not easy to understand so it will take practise. Years for some but it does not matter so long as you are working at the goal. Beware of outside interferences and some that want you to believe their version. Still respect them and recognise that is where they are. Today you got word again about being organized and getting ready for the next chapter. Many would have given up by now and when tired it would been so easy. Take a break and remember your pathway. We know how quick you will recover your strength again. Let us do it for you. The writing you are doing will help so many that are looking for answers. There are many ways that lead to Rome as the saying goes. You promised before you were born would best be advised to follow through.

Eternally yours. Courage. TttA

SAFE IN OUR MIDST!

Always feel guarded and safe when you are working or resting. Feel that is so. Today you did experience similar situations. The public is full of entities and so many carry grief and anger so you pick up too much from them. Try to remember to ask for extra protection when you are dealing with yourself and others. We are only reminding you about what you already know, but a little recall is healthy. So much is going on in so many different levels. So by trying to keep them apart can be trying. You do try, and at times you try too hard. All the practical advice and examples will also clarify what's going on. Your priorities are changing slightly but that is because your life is altering gradually. To assume what's happening is not always the best, so ask us first. To seek solitude is quite often one way to solve the problem. Withdrawal from crowds is not always easy but goes when you have to. Your books are going out in the right time and will be accepted.

Lots of love and support. TttA

LET LIFE FLOW!

Yes that is one way to let you know how everything flows. Pause is still valid but let your life stagnate. Inflow and outflow is also to be remembered. Young and old energies are mixed to make a balance. At times there is only one kind so look for one more input. When you have your class you feel it and know how different levels of learning are present. That is to remind of many levels of knowledge and acceptance of our wisdom. When we give you an answer in one way it's the quickest way for you to understand. Others will also have signs and changes that is the best way for them at that time. We know the spirit of each person in full so that is why we apply their cure and energy to each one in their own interest. Today you will reconnect with old friends again. So much time has gone and that was also prearranged. Go with our strength and love. Keep it flowing and growing.

Love and light TttA

LET THE HARMONY OF THE MUSIC FILL YOUR SOUL!

To understand that the sound of music is healing, uplifting and restoring is indeed a gift that you have often used in your kind of work. Look at it as a tool that is aiding in the deeper sense of all healing for soul, mind, body and emotions many gifted voice throughout the history and so many composers have indeed helped mankind up and enlighten so many sad hearts. All you that are gifted in one way or the other use your gifts for all including yourself. Healing with sounds is not new. Throughout the ages it has been used in sounds of a bell small and big and all instruments have a very big part also. Also remember what you play and listen to stays in the walls for ever. Used that as a sign when you enter a room. Stop and think how does it feel? The finer you are tunes in the faster you know. Practise and practise and you are getting there. It's all a big long lesson to enjoy, learn and teach others.

Blessings and eternal love. TttA

CALM AND TRUST WITH SURRENDER!

In these days when all the changes are occurring you need to stay extra calm and believe that we are in charge, and all is going to plan. Down through the ages it has happened time and time again. That is a part of learning and that part of learning and you can look and study to see the pattern. Try to be outside when possible to get the warm from the sun and all that natural energy. The slight breeze that you are feeling is also freshening things up. The week that has been was very helpful to you. We did send practical help also one more student. Your own welfare is being seen to and more work will be coming in for you to practise what we have taught you. We do understand your feelings about life better than anyone else. Too many times in the war zone made you very cautious but not daunting. The music you use is also benefitting you. Play some more. The old pattern was trying to stop you once again you were made aware of the sabotage made towards you.

Blessings and peace. TttA

ANOTHER DAY-ANOTHER CONNECTION!

Let our love and energy help, love and guide you throughout your day. No one is really capable of doing work for us by themselves. The work is done and will be forever done through you from us. Always remember where your strength comes from and where you go in the end of the day. The law of supply is eternal and you can count on us for every need. As we always have said surrender to us for next 24 hours and ask for us to lead and assist. The heavenly hosts are waiting to hear your voice. They will not act before you ask them. Pray to God for enlightenment and healing. The help is there but often not getting through because of lack of communication or the world is crowding in too much. Let our wisdom penetrate your work, life and your decisions. The big picture is unfolding so guard your spirit and mind. Thank you for doing your part in the big quest.

Amen to that. TttA

STAY FIRM AND CALM!

Let's stay together today and always. Together we will conquer and grow. Go on with today's work and do as much as you are able. We know that you are always doing so. Take care of not underdoing or overdoing any situation. It could easily happen when you are tired or not focused. You are learning and practising every day, so keep up the good work. Today you have had another big test. It will get easier as you go along and spot the actions and what's going on. The cold weather is also making things harder to get more work done. But it's only for a short time. Yesterday was a turning point towards the light. The seasons are forever coming and going. Later on it will be a different climate. Only slowly so you humans can get used to it better than before. Let the days go by taking in one day at the time. Too much is going on at the same time. For now spread your work out and rest in between. Courage and healing from us all.

Eternal blessing and joy. TttA

ALL IN GOOD TIME!

As you already know, things happen when it is divine timing. Nothing to do with Earthly time. It has to fit in with all concerned, and how much is understood. Last night you felt us helping and uplifting all of you. It was a peaceful and healing session. As you know there was some interference, but you did ask us to deal with it so the outcome was fine. Your health is improving and it has been a long time to get as far as you have. The cooperation and time with us has done a great job. All is not quite 100% yet but we are doing our best to speed it up. It's been a lot to understand out of the ordinary ways of thinking, but you are opening your eyes a lot wider. Day by day you are adding one more page to your book of life. Many have not trusted or believed you but tongues have been wagging. The truth will come out to the end. Today you will have more work on many levels, so stay firm and detached afterwards. Let go of tomorrow's thoughts.

Blessings in full measure. TttA

ETERNAL LAW AND SUPPLY!

Let us deal with all supplies. Only by requests can you leave all small and big situations to us. We know, but you still have to ask for help before we can give it to you all. Let it be known to many when healing is needed down on Earth and for the planet itself. Throughout the ages we have been watching the wars and peace in so many places. Lately you have been aware of so many changes in so many and we are showing you every day. Your trust in us is much improved because you have seen much more of your work come alive through us. The waiting is very frustrating but it did teach you patience and compassion. Also you have learnt to detach better from situations that was for us to finish off. It's cooperation on many levels and you have seen that, so keep on doing as you are until more wisdom can be given. We are making sure that you are prepared. Thank you for trying and for your persistence.

Amen and blessings. TttA

JOY FOR EVER MORE!

Let joy flow throughout your being and spread the joy to all. So many are trying to do so are afraid or hesitant if not knowing exactly what to do and when. It gets left or half-heartedly done. More joy, less stress and it will go into the physical system and cause ill health but you know that already so we are once more reminding you to tell others. Your part is being upgraded because you have seen and heard more, so you can understand how it all works. Today's work with the old Lemurian will have beneficial consequences for you both. Old connections will re surface. Blessings of the highest order and wisdom for days to come and will ripple in to families and situations. We are behind you and we are doing all the concerning and healing work that's needed. Let the blessings of the day stay with you always and you will also feel better by being activated again and complete.

Calming and loving thoughts. TttA

BLESSINGS AND LOVE!

The last few days you all got some blessings from the stars that also involves us. We are connected to the universal pattern and all is and all is working in union. We have seen the miracles on Earth eventuate. We needed someone with a solid faith to anchor down, so more healing, understanding and balancing could be activated. You are in the beginning of a new face of work. We have told you so but not when. Now you know a little more of our wisdom so you trust more. It's all about building and learning under your journey through out your lifetimes. Let today be a day of thankfulness and praise. We like some love and light to come back to us also. Charred energy and love is helping the universal kingdom. Blessings from the star system and lots of love and light to all. Many will accept others will not. Let that give you a guideline. You only have to ask us and then listen in.

TttA

GIVE THE GLORY TO THE FATHER!

Always remember where the source is. No one would do anything by themselves of any value if you don't connect. It's all as we have said so many times a matter of cooperation and trust. We need you as much as you need us for a great input. Day by day you are noticing changes in people and situations. You could feel it's starting so it was at times a situation. Your work is being noticed by us and more will come. You are also getting more of input balancing and healing is really the same thing. Carry out what's on your plate today. One more situation to help will be coming later on for you to do our work. You are an anchor on Earth to help and stabilise and balance out conditions. Little by little the work that you provided is being done. Like the old story brick by brick the fort will be a stronghold to rely on. Let our guiding light be uplifting throughout your day. Have little just be in time between so that will help you to balance your energy level. Spend a little time outside when possible. The natural energies will restore you and make your life more positive and cheerful.

Eternal blessings and cheers from us all. TttA

RENEWAL

The old, no longer useful, will be replaced. That is a good thing. To be able to have a replacement and new growth is the promise that we have made to you so long ago.

We are doing the best for you as fast as we can because of the complex system. It needs to be done in sections. Too much too soon will not benefit you as a whole. Leave all your questions and we are doing and we are doing all the protection we can. Unwind today and be outside whenever possible. The nature is revitalising and uplifting you so you are able to do your work as it has started on a new chapter. It will be very good for you and a lot of help for other people. Your new workload will spread out so you will have to rest in between. We are your teachers and healers so we know all and act accordingly. Trust in the source and enjoy having a team as strong as we are. Love laugh and relax. All is indeed well. We know how you feel and your whole system is getting an overhaul.

Blessings and love in hundred fold. TttA

A new day!

My children of light it's really a new day. Every day you have been practising that now for a long time. Let's look at it as a learning time and another lesson. So much time is being used to think about yesterday and yester years. It's only to learn from and then carry on to learn more. Many times people don't see the point as to why it is happening so nothing will change. Then another situation more obvious then the first will occur until the pattern is clear. It's hard for many including for yourself throughout the year. If anyone is too close to the situation it will not be seen clearly. Anyway just a reminder to think about. Life is changing for the better after yesterday's sort out so enjoy what comes and we are still guarding you and your work, also making sure that the trust is working. The information given to you today is true and valid. The activation has already started. Give thanks to all concerned. Remember to first have the spirit line clear and in charge. More tomorrow.

Blessings from us all and blessings for your mother's big day. TttA

ORDER!

Let the order in your life help you to see the bigger picture and also it will save time and energy. Do delay any suggestions. Deal with only two things at a time. When tools and other aids are ready to use you will know the time to start to use them again. Take the signs as a prompting from us to get going and carry out our work on Earth with our help and to help to fulfil the destiny of our master plan. Today you have seen more of just that. When things fall in to place that are meant to be. Other times it gets stopped or something more important has taken the priority. All is forever changing and altering to suit the situation .Stand by and get ready for more work Your willingness to cooperate strengthen the bond and gladdens our heart. To be willing to see and hear and experience so much is indeed something to be grateful for. Count your blessings and smile with a joyful heart. Talk to whomever you need to and always ask for our guidance.

Lots of love and blessings. TttA

CONNECTION TO THE SOURCE!

Let the connection be very close and solid to us. At present time so much is getting activated and so there could easily be distractions or side-tracking's going on. Today's work is being activated and it was already on the map. A long time ago the chief wanted to test and connect with his own and set things right. The situation was old and he was looking for an anchor on Earth to get it all sorted so he could advance and work on his spiritual path, for his own good and for fauna. Many old situations are being balanced and whoever is being used was working as a tool. Other tools will also be given to aid the cause of old misdeeds and for old long time forgotten events. Let today's meeting be beneficial for all concerned. Relax and enjoy for the rest of the time that will be good for your balance. You said you wanted more work so it's coming to your door. You are well thought of by many so we have cleared your deck for the peace and harmony to work for you. Get on with your work and you are getting it all together in all four areas.

Believe and be glad. TttA

SPEAK OF OUR TRUTH!

My children keep on speaking the truth-whatever tries to hinder you. The truth will always prevail and the truth will set you free, and whatever or whomever will try to daunt you but it will never work. Thank you for carrying out your part and in return we are healing, guiding and renewing you. The gems that you are using as tools will enhance and accelerate the healing or balancing up whatever is out of time. The events yesterday were meant to alert you to what is still going on. One fine day it will clear and your work will increase and bear fruit. Rather it's our work that you are passing on and remember the scribe is making it available to the public. Think of your part as a service to the source. You will see more results soon. Changing times are here so change will come also in to your life. The sort out time is still present so the main part is done. Little alteration will still be present- but you will feel it ahead. Stay with the program for now. All is indeed working very well. Thank you.

Love and light. TttA

IN THE STILLNESS OF THE AFTERNOON!

Listen in and hear our voice speaking to you from nature. The birds and the plants are telling you a story. Touch and look in to a flower or tune in to an animals thoughts. They both will tell you what's going on in their world. Some searching souls will also come for peace and healing. As your home is our home we will invite the ones that need it most. If nothing seems to happen just wait and get ready. That is the seasons of work and training in patience and focus. You have seen all that happening so pass it on. Today clearing of thoughts will be very beneficial for both of you. Next week will bring unexpected work for you, we advise you to do it. Still remember your own progress. It has taken time but you are advancing rather the Earth-so you can enjoy more of your garden. Keep your regime going and don't for one day give up. Have a rest or just be. Keep on asking for help-when things get too much.

Blessings and healing with love. TttA

KEEP OUR SPECIAL TIME!

To be able to keep our times for connection and communication takes discipline and focus. At times you get side tracked, but less than before so keep on working on it. The more discipline and patience you get the more work you will have. Still keep your balance so all areas will unite. Let go of a few more situations that were here to test you and then leave it to us. You now have feelings and just know where things are and in which direction. Still check and let us guide you throughout your journey in time and space. Let the day unfold as it may. The unfolding of time is here so open up to receive. Also keep up your regime. It's of value that you follow through. One more month and a new order will be given. In the meantime do what's on your plate. Send more love and light to your fellow man. We are all behind you. Yesterday's call was a great healing time.

Loving thoughts from TttA

STAY FIRM AND JOYFUL!

So much is trying to influence so many about decisions and so called truths. Beware of the ones that say they know it all. Many know part of the truth. Some do more than all others. Detach and cut when you feel uneasy about anyone or anything. Temptation always leads to control. To be able to stay clear of situations and well-meaning people if you find the motive is not acceptable. You gain more when you keep an eye on the situation from afar. Much too often people get too close to the picture and will not be seen. Your gut feeling is still operating so use that when you feel what way it really is. Stay firm when the wind blows and storm rages. It depends on your root system. How strong it is and how firm the ground is and is it firm enough? Most that are working for a goal will be tested and tried many times, as you have experienced before. Keep on working and take life as it comes. Things will be sorted in good time.

Cheers and health. TttA

REFRESHMENT TIME!

To be able to refresh when needed is indeed a good thing. When the feeling to do something is strong, check and ask when and how. Go ahead with your plans today and enjoy the little things as well as the big things. Your work for us is changing and so are you, to be able to do what you are trained for. Many years now we have tested and taught you many things and you are indeed learning fast. Let us be around you and make the evening turn out as it should. All was planned and you were given all the tools necessary for what's coming. Everyone draws people to themselves because of the thoughts they are sending out. Keep that in mind for further reference and keep focused, occupied and joyful as possible. Time will tell you what next. All in good time. The universal picture is forever changing because of the ever moving living planets. All in their own particular path and all in order. God's plan is very well organized.

Amen to that and thank you. TttA

TO KNOW IS GOOD-BUT NOT ENOUGH. TO BE WISE IS THE ANSWER!

The wisdom is to know when to do what. Learn and study from life. You all need to have another look at how your actions and thoughts got you to many places but how was the end result. Many questions have been asked for a long time. That is a healthy sign and you will get your answers. A short time as you already know. In the meantime carry out your duties and work with discipline and focus. To have sharp eyes like a hawk and hear with both ears will help you to understand the situations. Keep going as you are to have sharp eyes like a hawk and hear with both ears will help you to understand the situations that arise. Keep going as you are the main work situation educated by us is indeed a very privileged task. Many would have left years ago. Still we say rest and recharge when it calls for. Plenty of clearing goes on and you have noticed the alterations. Keep going as you are the main situations are being dealt with including the daily healing, Input and advice.

Enjoy today and give thanks. TttA

PEACE AND BALANCE!

Let our peace and balance come in to the very core of the matter. The light and love will clarify what's going on. To shine a light in to dark corner is indeed very important. The dark murky waters of residue from the past years and life will be disbursed with the energy from the source. Never think that you cannot do or accomplish all without our help. We are a team and will stay so forever. You are one of us now so we treat you as a member of the unit. The sun today will help you lighten your thoughts and soul and by keeping up your regime you will conquer. Keep going and don't look back. Tomorrow will soon come and we will prepare you for next task. Yesterday's talk was an old connection from Tibet. It will be good for you to connect again. Work in coordination and order. You are being led and still tested. That is because you must be ready and you nearly are. Hard at times but beneficial in the long term. Today's task will be dealt with and you will get your answers.

Blessings and health from all of us. TttA

AT LAST!

We have been waiting for you a very long time. The connection is still there but circumstances have been very severe. Well now have a fresh start and do rejoice for a chance of being able to work and grow. The sun is still shining again on you and in you. Many have tried to dim your news. That was because of your future works will expose many of so called workers. That is not really your work only let us know what's on your plate. Calm and peace will enter you and your place again. We are very aware what you are dealing with and all your changes in all four areas. Some people are thinking that they know you, only what they think is not there anymore so take that in to your consideration when communicating with them. We will help you to straighten them out about you. The sun will invigorate today and get you further on your journey. We are very close by and you only have to ask for us and we will be there in an instant. Blessings for the day.

Amen and courage. TttA

ALL BACK TOGETHER!

Let the union stay strong and very flexible. To bend is fine but watch out for strong wind or a disturbing whirlwind. You feel what's going on and now take actions to prepare yourself and others. Last few weeks has shown you all about people and their ways and how to handle things. That does fully show you who they are and how much is not understood by them. Back to the old saying you can't give beef to a baby. The afternoon's sun will aid your feelings of wellbeing and strengthen you before you get on with your new assignment. Slowly and safely in your case. A gradual opening up of your picture will also show you the wider screen, and lighten up your world. Your beliefs and decisions are right on track. Keep up the work. To explain to others is not always good. Very few will accept our teachings. Isolation is good at times but not for too long. Your time will come and you will be made new. You have asked many questions and we have responded in our ways. Next month will tell a story and you will be surprised over the outcome.

Blessings and courage. TttA

ETERNAL BLESSINGS!

My children of light you are blessed, especially now when things are coming to a head. The big sort out time is here and you have felt it for a long time now always ahead so when we are telling you, you already know. The close feelings and love is very strong, and becoming stronger. The testing time is here so you also being checked over in all areas. At times you have wondered and asked, because of the work you are doing. Certain things that needed to clear and got rid of. Well now that is alone only a few more days and you will like renewed and ready again. We are always close and we understand exactly how things are. Now you soon can operate whatever is called for. The big alterations are here and you will be delighted to see, hear and feel all that is coming to you. Beware we will make all things new. Miracles still happen and for you and it will feel like that for you have had many revelations so far and more will be given.

Courage, love and joy from us all. TttA

IN THE EARLY HOURS
OF THE MORNING!

Let's stay close and loving, so much depends on the connection between us. You know how many would like to part us. It's been a big task for you this year. You are still here and stronger for it. Rejoice and keep up the good work. We are there right behind you. You feel the sort out and are concerned at the speed many times. Relax and do your recharging with our help. Most people don't fully understand how important it all is. It's not a make believe or game. It's worldwide and universal. Look at the big picture and ask us where you fit in with your work. It's really our work and you are a piece of the chain of work. Today is a new feeling of change. All has its own timing and actions. Today will unfold as we see fit. When you surrender you leave all to us and we make sure that all is in good working order. You are now into a new way of expressions. The alterations that are done to you are now activated. You also have had stronger premonitions about many situations.it will save you time and energy.

Courage and eternal love. TttA

CARRY ON!

Let's do just that together. The togetherness today needs to be improved and clarified. You as well as many other light workers would do well to understand the importance of unity. Still be alone and keep up your time with us. The discipline with all your spirit work is your first commitment when that is done all other areas will be sorted out and dealt with. Many work opposite and will get opposite results. That stands to reason and when you are practical you will see things faster. The speed of it all now is past most people's understanding. So take a day at a time and follow through. You are growing in grace and we fully support you. The storm has been raging for a long time remember not to break but stay flexible, as bending will make you see what's going on. See both sides of the story. The human heart is so delicate at times so thread very carefully. Tonight is one more healing time with us. We will give you all the energy and healing tools.

Blessings. TttA

RENEW AND REFRESH!

To be able to do so before the spring is to get prepared. Always prepare and hope for a better tomorrow. It's not up to others what you feel and do. It's up to you how you feel and think towards yourself and others. Others could influence you and if you don't ask don't take their advice on board. Many are very willing to alter your ways but instead it would be advisable to look in to their own behaviour. Many will learn others just look and listen but never understand. Leave them to us and carry on connecting with new souls. The big sort out is still on going and you are feeling the effect very strongly. Bear with it and rejoice when you have one more opportunity for every day to work for the source. You have been experiencing a lot lately, that's only for your growth and evolvement. Still remember why you are here and why your teaching is very timely Stay close to the source and be aware who is entering your sanctuary. You are always loved and protected from all harm.

Blessings TttA

BEWARE I MAKE ALL THINGS NEW!

My beloved children of light, miracles still happen and we are still in charge. Many have stopped to believe and become materialised and only believe what they can see. Many will alter and start to hear and experience many new things. Like the weather that can change in an instant, the same with people. The only things that you are responsible for is you. It's not a helping hand to do others work. In an emergency fine. Let the guiding light show you how much to say. We know that the human souls are delicately made up so don't so don't do more than you are asked from us. You still are going through some experiences that are new to you. Stay patient calm and joyful as much as possible. Try to leave it all to us. Your system is very complex so ordinary help is not suitable. All is so well as possible and this month will sort it's self out. We will make it so easy on you as possible so you can recharge and go back to work full speed.

Our blessings and love with healing. TttA

CARRY ON!

Please do just that. Progress has been made lately. You have learned a valuable lesson. Whatever comes now you are better prepared. It's very hard times for many souls. The pressure to stay on your path is a great test. Don't despair; only take a day at a time. All changing circumstances are aiding the shift to make it easier for you to make work satisfactory and less energy will be used. The time is getting shorter day by day so use it for your spirit work for yourself and all mankind. It will always be some that will fall in to stony hearts and minds. That is not your responsibility, leave all that to us. You are now at a stage when you can see and hear more. Use this time to rethink, recharge and renew yourself. Let the day unfold as we have your best interest for your wellbeing. Soon it will clear and you will feel when because of your input in the healing work. We are giving you all you need for each soul. Your system is indeed getting renewed. Trust and faith is there.

Courage and joy. TttA

HEALING AND LETTING GO!

Let our technical team use our advanced methods on you and the one that enters your home. The ones that are advancing will have to deal with more karma. The higher you go the better you are equipped to deal with a deeper level of forgiveness. It's not an easy lesson to learn, but you are doing so as much as you are able to do. The days of healing are quite severe but it had to be because of the serious event in so many past lives. Look and learn to be able to put it all behind you once and for all. Next lesson will be easier and not so draining. Forever growing and learning will add to your understanding of life on a very deep level. When you do that you are able to help man kind and explain what's going on. The signs and guidelines from the source will also clarify about safe travels and how to safely get to your goals. Trust that all tools will be given in plenty of time. Surrender morning and night.

Blessings and healing. TttA

A NEW DAY!

Yes, it's a new day every day. Make the most of it and do not over or underdo anything. You of all people will know how important that is. To keep a balance at present time is very hard. The best thing anyone can do is to slowly make way for a new life. Too much of anything is not good for anyone. Look at the sun is rising every day and how much brighter life seems to be when a ray of light comes in to your life. Soon it will be a new input so in the meantime get ready. All is in divine time so it will take its course. It's time for work and it's time for play and rest. Let that pattern get you through these times. Don't compare with others. That's not for you so live your own life as best way as possible. Enjoy the warmth today from the winter sun. You are improving with wisdom, health and joy in small measures for now but bigger later. Everything starts in a small version and grows from there. We still love and care for you and you can trust that our judgement is for the best for all.

Courage and love. TttA

EVERY DAY- A FRESH START!

For so many years we have told you just that. Many times you have done so other times many different issues have come up. Remind yourself about facts and illusions. Many times it could appear back to front. If you feel any unease, then stop and ask us for a check. Some people are really experts about the version of illusions and at times they are ruled by other influences. Stay very clear of make beliefs and fakes, you have seen enough of them all and what it can do to people and situations. Take time out when the need arises and do absolutely nothing. Just to be its all you want many times. Plenty of healing last night and today as we are with you once again. Later on you will experience more of what some bring with them, and how does it make you feel? Ask yourself what you are learning from it all. As you now know it is getting stronger and every day we will prepare you for more work and more time out. Tonight is a time for grace and harmony together with us. We are rejoicing with you for every step taken in faith.

Blessings TttA

LOVE YOURSELF!

Love every cell in your body. All cells are intelligent and will respond to your thoughts and actions. Do be aware of negativity and destructive behaviour. The daily communication and love sent to your body is trying very hard under the circumstances behind normal patterns. Many physical items would not have appeared if more care and love had been transmitted to all cells. The whole structure of the human body is under review and needs to be looked at much further. The many techniques that already exist on Earth are all beneficial. Choose the one that is suitable for you. Relax and meditate. Don't be discouraged if it takes time. Many humans have medical expressions from the alterations from their bodies. Stay positive and don't expect the same time in all cases so different for some. It's very personal so the pattern of treatment will be the same.

Blessings until tomorrow. Archangel Uriel. TttA

BELOVED CHILDREN!

Let us heal you all from past trauma and distress. We are a very big team of angels ready to assist you all in all sorts and conditions. That has been coming on for years. Many situations have been avoided but too much was going on at the time. To be able to clear all we need your cooperation. Many have suffered unduly because they have taken on others feelings and thoughts. Many times we have told you to leave it to us. We have been watching over you for a long time and your own situation is from past years before Earth and afterwards. All of that is now clearing and you need to be trusting a little more. We have it all in our hands and the complex situations are only for us and we can use our technique to speed it all up. You need to feel loved healed and joyful. That will come soon. Wait if you say wait.

Eternal blessings and love, thank you. TttA

TRUST AND FAITH!

In these days you would be wise to use the two words for getting you though. Many go to many places and some get a big bunch of ideas of what to do and when. We say surrender and leave it all to us to sort out and give you advice about the situations. First be calm and empty out and then we can tell you and you will get on the right path for enlightenment of your work and where to connect to or join in. You have seen so many times and energy trying to act on your own. Make sure that you have a positive team on your link. Many times in stormy weather it would be wise until the peace has returned once again. Timing is very important because you will have delays if you act too soon. Relax and try to see the guidance and law behind every action. All in good time and remember to stay close to us.

Amen and health with joy. TttA

STAY CLOSE TO THE SOURCE!

Stay very near and you will feel the power and the love from us. If you are not sure, ask and you will hear us calling you from our fort. The fort is a stronghold for seafarers and whalers but went too far away for them to hear my voice. That is one way you will picture in your mind also your lighthouse that has been burning for so long time. We're activating your tools so you can get a faster connection. These days you have been given a stronger bond so you can feel and see us faster. The big healing last night was indeed from us and you were privileged to have that from us through one of our healers on Earth. More will come and soon you will be better than you ever have been. You have prayed for a long time and you did not get any replays. Now is the time for activation and show others the light. We have been guarding you and always will be, so be of good cheer.

Courage and love. TttA

ONE DAY AT A TIME!

Let go once more about people and situations that's not as yet happened. We have told you every 24 hours and that we will look after you then until next 24 hours to sort everything out, but not too much will come at once and this will be very beneficial for all. The winter is still bringing you another view. The same goes for your life change, it's good to see what's going on. Some people want to be seen and heard so they keep on complaining about others to get attention. Most will also show a great need of lack of love and respect for themselves and others. All of that is very human but not very evolved. Send out more thoughts of compassion and universal love. The desperation of some is very obvious. Remember who you are and what you are. Stay very flexible and do cheer up for these times are only temporary. Express the truth to all in words actions and thoughts. You know which one that will apply to whom. Get a few things done and remember to just be in between.

Loving and good thoughts from TttA

TRANQUILLITY!

Let us supply all that to you all in these trying times. So much is changing and so many are and so many are feeling the effects of it all. Some get it in the physical and others in the spiritual, mental and emotional areas. Whatever is the weakest part in each person's system. Alterations are being made so all will be well to the end. Nature and life are doing their part in healing it all. Many think differently but that is not for you to get involved in. Opinions are good as long as you check the real reasons. Let go a little more about ifs and buts. Only do what's on your plate, for each day. Keep as warm and happy as possible. Your new music will also aid for calm and relaxing feelings for all that's coming to your place. Last night's connection was very valid. The woman will have a new start and she will know where to go, also helping many young souls to see what love is. Keep on going in your own speed and stronghold.

Many loving thoughts to you all. TttA

PERFECT PEACE!

Enjoy your peace inside your loving heart. It will help you to love others. Many are looking in the wrong places and searching for you and your sanctuary. We will make sure that your place and surroundings are suitable for all the ones that find you. The world is filled with so many alternatives and solutions. The only one to find is the source and stay close for more learning. All the interruptions are there to test you and your work. You are now doing very well, particularly when we are around you more. Let that picture stay in your mind and let us do the work. You are still doing your part, but in a better balanced way. Rejoice with us and the angels about how far you have come and with so much more understanding. Your health is steadily improving and so will your work. Many hurdles have been overcome and your wisdom is greater. Stay strong and vigilant.

Many rich rewards from us. Thank you. TttA

LET THE PAST STAY IN THE PAST!

To go over past mistakes and ground is not good for anyone. Learn from it and be aware of what to do next time. If this not always clear, then guidelines are obvious, look again and dig deeper. Try to stand back when you feel too close. The third way is to get up high and get a bird's eye view of the situation. The time will soon pass and a new dawn will come and all of you that have been exhausted or disheartened will renew their strength and start again. The preparation time has been very severe this time. Many have suffered psychically or in other areas of importance. That will help you to understand how life is. Stand by today and very close for your assistance on different dimensions. In our midst are also many that need love and light. We all have been overstressed after so much sorting and aiding. We all need you on Earth to do your part and hold the energy as much as you can. Rest in between and work as you are.

God bless and keep you. TttA

MYSTERIES TO BE REVILED!

Many queries will get answers that have been in a mist for a long time. It's again to be told the old wisdom about timing. All in its right time, so wait for yours. You will know beforehand, so relax and let life flow. If you are feeling uneasy it's certainly shadows about. Your body is the best barometer. Still we say check and wait until we give you one more clue. Little by little it will unfold so go with the flow. Days when nothing eventful is occurring and days when all things are coming together behind the scenes. There are brighter times ahead so look forward to more warmth and light. You all need to experience many new things and many new feelings. Emotions are still a good guideline so detach and do what's needed for the day. Go ahead with improvements in a way that will enhance your life and others. Still get your priorities in order to be able to get all done. That's on your plate. Eternal blessings from us all in all dimensions.

Courage and light from an extra strong beam. TttA

KEEP ON SORTING OUT!

A little at a time will get you in to order and picture that you want. Make a time each day for joy, work and rest. Just the same as you are building a wall one brick at the time will make a stronghold, today's work will be a preparation for tomorrows joy. The same for your spirit work. Keep-on going to all things done of the work we have given you. When one lesson has been learned you will advance to next level. If at first you don't see or understand, stand back or rise above it. We have told you so many times and we still will let you know when the need is there. Try to live as simple and natural so it will be less energy used. Be careful how you use your wisdom trust and energy as too many would like to take without thinking how to give something back. Leave all of them behind you and look for fresh new input. We have heard your request and we will deal with it in the best way as possible.

More tomorrow from all of us. TttA

REJOICE!

Let's come together and enjoy each other's company for a short while. Life at present is a mystery and for some hard to cope with. Just carry on as you have begun and you will be able to handle just about anything. People will react to you in many different ways, only because where they are. Don't concern yourself with their pathway, its nothing to do with you when you are being asked to connect with us and do what is required. To be able to follow through is essential. You have known that for some time, but we needed to remind you today. As it stands now you are able to be free to act and rest when it is the right time. It was a hard and necessary decision for your growth. You have now come a little further along your path. Many years of letting go and digging deeper. Carry out our wishes and do the best you can as we know that you are able. Welcome the new peace and quiet.

Amen to all that TttA

PEACE IS COMING!

Nothing is better for growth and health for peace of soul, mind and body and emotions. You have seen so much damage that could have been avoided if only peace was present. Learn from it and don't look back. Today you also have been aware of group work and how important that is that harmony and peace is present. Calm and joy will also enhance your progress. Also so much energy will be spent not having to ask queries and deal with unease. Soon you will notice the changes in your life. It's quite severe but necessary. People and situations will still take some of your time. More time spent with healing and teaching. In these times you need a balance of energies present, if not the atmosphere will soon show unease. Many souls are very sensitive so go easy on the ones that come. When in doubt ask us. Still be vigilant and aware. People are so blind and hypnotised so the illusion is very dangerous. Stand back and let us deal with the problem. Stay calm and free as much as possible. You will succeed and come out on top as we already have told you.

Blessings and love. TttA

WITHDRAWAL TIME!

These times are essential for your growth. All should do well to follow that example. You know so well what will happen when you dismiss these thoughts. Back to balance again. So much better health when you follow good advice. Let go of yesteryears once and for all. No one can destroy you no matter how hard they try. We are your keeper's guardians and friends and very soon you will experience what you have been asking for for such a long time. Patiently you have been waiting for the time to pass and used it for the course. You will now always work for us and many others will follow. The others are not ready. We are looking for a solution for other subjects that are too complicated for you to deal with. Blessings be upon you for now and forever. Today will bring you some good news that you have been waiting for.

Love and light for all that are working for us. TttA

WE ARE VERY CLOSE!

Today you will experience a lot of peace and joy. Maybe not what you have thought about so don't make any important plans just yet. Many conditions are being seen to so let us do what we are here to do. Your conditions are complex so it has taken a lot of years to put things in order. Be patient with us, as we are with you. Because of so many different aspect of life band your type of work it has been very severe and we are doing everything in our mighty powers to speed things up. Healing is given to all that are asking. The same again we ask you not to make your own decisions without not comparing with us. The mighty onslaught is mental physical, emotional and spiritual what's going on. Not everyone is in the front line but you all are feeling the signs of battle scarring on my children but soon you will feel more secure and at ease again. The longing for all other areas to get balanced is also getting looked at. The cold season is also taking its toll. Stay close and you will be right.

Blessings and courage. TttA

WONDERS WILL UNFOLD!

Believe and it will happen. So much trauma and unease for such a long time has made you so weary and you need to recharge for a little longer. The healing you are getting every night and all extras is speeding up your strength and energy levels. It's been so hard for many times so you feel like just resting. That's O.K. but slowly you are regaining a new vision. Only a little at a time so you can digest it all. Too much for a long time will get you exhausted. So easy does it. Be ever so steady and vigilant. Still remember one day at a time it's all you have to deal with. Keep warm and calm. We will make sure that you have all the assistance that you want. Lately you have wondered what next and how that is for us to decide. Many people that mean well-but don't know you so the advice is not very valid. They only see what they want to see because you appear to many in so many variations of life. Today is another day so treat it as such. Patience and surrender is still to be worked at.

Blessings and health. TttA

JUST KNOW THAT ALL IS WELL!

Belief and trust are also two more keys to know that we are looking after your welfare and supporting your work on all levels. Many times you have asked and wondered how much longer you have to wait before you can see progress. We have already seen the work that's been done in your place, and for you to see more. Sit quiet and breathe in slowly and we will put the picture in your mind so you will be able to understand all work that has been done in other dimensions. Also as the sun is now more visible you will enjoy sitting in your garden and feeling the energy returning to you. Let us keep you in our care and keep on cooperating with the input we give you daily. Nature is indeed an excellent healer and you know that but sometimes you need to be reminded. The new growth in your garden will remind you about your own growth after all study retreat and healing done in our name. You still are trying very hard to get a few more tasks done, that will change and the energy also. To renew a few items and get things shifted also helps. Discard what's not needed it will make more room for new situations.

Keep up the good work. TttA

CALM IN THE STORM!

Let my peace come over you and enfold you to make you feel and experience a lot of my joy, calm and peace. At the present time it's a holy war going on, so stay as steady and positive as possible. Storm and rage with unease will recede. You know that is so except times you are so sensitive so you multiply the severity of it and that cause you to have more psychical symptoms than many others. You have asked for all that to stop and it is so. No prayers get unanswered it takes time once in a while to activate so stay with the thoughts that we have given you and the angels are also assisting you in so many ways. Today is the last day of the month so let it all be gone and be forgotten. All the work you are doing will bear fruit soon. Stay with only calm and positive people. You will not perish. All happens in the right time according to the blueprint.

Courage and strength from all of us. Cheer up you are doing fine. TttA

A NEW DAY!

Yes my children of light it's a new day every day. Yesterday has gone and has been learnt from. The warm weather has begun to return and you felt more alive. That's the good energy from the source and our love for you and all that is working on the protection for guardian ship and healing both for humanity and Mother Earth. One always affects the other so live in union and harmony as much as possible. If anything occurs that's for you deal with that at once. The last few days has shown you what's needed to be done, and it got done. Now is the time when nature is waking up and pets and the birds that survived the winter. They have started to make nests and singing more at twilight. Enjoy your meeting today and send your blessings to all the divas that are living in your garden and you will feel that connection more later on and at times you will see them as we have noticed your strong nature connections. Keep that going and send love and light to all living things.

Eternal blessings TttA

HOLY-HOLY-HOLY!

Today is the day to awaken so many entrapped souls and to expose lechers and monkey business. God and the angels don't look favourable on these situations. Every soul has their own journey and own work. The only way to grow is to study, have discipline and be focused. I have seen too many times how it affects people that allow themselves to be drained or just spirit abused. The nurturing and love from the source will support you and act as a guide for your long and winding journey. At times you can act as a starting button and then let go for the work being done in every ones best interest for involvement with the higher power. And so it goes on. Still be responsible for thoughts and actions and the wisdom given out so you can add that to your knowledge about life in the present dimension. Keep on looking after your wisdom and how it can be used for the good of all mankind.

Amen to that. TttA

SOAK UP THE ENERGIES IN YOUR GARDEN!

Enjoy the growth and life forces from the plants, animals and nature spirits. All living things are a gift from God. Give thanks and gratitude for every day you are living and remember to nurture and love yourself. Go ahead and relax with the inspired to do. All of you have different talents and will enjoy different activities so remember the individuals are doing what's natural to them. Ask us when you don't know what to do with some people. Many are trying to get a piece of the cake mainly an energy drain from the person that brings it down from the source. Beware to see who is who and be an onlooker. To stand back is also beneficial.

The last few days you have discovered many mysteries that you already knew but not all the details. It needed to be the right time for the situation to be exposed for what it really is. The grades of so many is psychics are growing but that no value only a beginning, that could lead them to become spiritual which is the only thing that helps anyone's growth and understanding.

Blessings for the day and night. Good work done. TttA

RECHARGE FROM THE SOURCE!

It's of most important value that you check and get the right time information so that you can help and enlighten others that we send to you. So many pretend to be from the source who never intended to be. The subtle approach is quite give a way so if anything doesn't feel right leave it alone. Many would love to see you fall and stop doing your duty and keep your promise that you have made such a long time ago. Extra protection will be given each time you ask. It's so severe at present so all our teams and helpers with assistance are occupied. You have experience so much lately so go easy on yourself. All that challenge is to help your work for the future. Joy and rest will get you back to 100% again. Still we say have faith and discipline as much as you can. Everything is getting sorted so rest in that reassurance. Stay in the sun for a while today and that will energise you once again. Always stay very close to us we will keep the unwanted ones out once and for all. Trust and relax we have all in hand.

Peace and wisdom. TttA

RAYS OF SUNSHINE!

Let my son and the sunny rays brighten your days. You all would do well to follow that advice. Still we say it's not an order, only advice. Go ahead and do what's needed for your daily quests. Enjoy the warmth and get refreshed in your garden of delight. At present quite a few colours are showing up and it will also give you pleasure. Keep on using colour therapy and tell others how to use it also. Let today be a peaceful and calm day to benefit many others. Everybody needs to take stock and understand the value of life and learning. Checking and double checking is needed at these times. Not long now and all will be revealed. Learning and loving is of help and will make you understand why and how so much is changing and coming to the surface. Break in slowly and feel the changes. Life is altering for the better so stay with your plan. No one knows better than you how it can be and why. Today will bring some news that you have been waiting for. Take it as a sign from universe. Be outside as much as possible and let life flow.

Eternal blessings from all your team. TttA

LET'S WORK TOGETHER!

United you stand against the onslaughts. Stay firm, calm and vigilant in all areas as much as possible. The energy field will be strengthened and all will benefit greatly. Spend time alone and also be in the green pastures. When you feel tired or neglected Mother Nature will always look after all that are looking after her. The same principles also apply to humans. Self-love and understanding of human nature is also helpful. Listen in and empty out what is not beneficial for you anymore. As you change so will your life in all areas. Colour and people in early days who were liked or were needed will no longer be suitable. Favour alterations or complete change. It will make the energy go round and not stagnate. Today is another day so be thankful you are getting wiser and healthier every day. Have faith and still be giving out love and light to all that you allow to enter your sanctuary. They hear you but have not taken it on board. Not wanting to change their ways for the better. Not your problem so send them to us to deal with but watch who is coming and whom they bring with them.

Lots of love and peaceful joy. TttA

STAY CLEAR OF NEGATIVITY!

Yes we say that again and again that you can never let go of keeping a stronghold of all energies and all that bring negativity. Ask them to try harder to be positive or leave.

So many sad souls are wanting love and light so do your part and lighten some ones burden. Many times you just have to listen and give them to us to deal with. Lately you have come across so many cases that needed, wanting and are stuck in an old thinking pattern. Let it all go it can be done and you are doing it as a good example. Also when they know that someone understands they get hope. Still somebody would like to trip you up but it is a waste of time in your case. All that support healing and knowledge you now have will sort that out. Keep on tuning in and working as you are. The month will soon go and then you will see a vast improvement. Tonight will be as s good as it can be. We will attend and do our work for all. Enjoy and relax as much as possible for the rest of the day.

Blessings and love to all. TttA

START AGAIN!

Let no one or any event hinder your progress and disturb you from doing your life purpose. You are strongly and perfectly protected so you can do all that is necessary for your part of the cleaning, teaching and healing. It's a new day so all are recharged and done to perfection. The weather is also a part of making your life so much easier. Bright and shiny energies comes out from your home and that is why at times you get spirit lecher's hanging around. Don't do the cleaning work yourself only ask us to deal with it at once. Rest and recharge for every day that's going and you are improving. More supporters will be entering your group and more will get access to the truth from us. Though you. Carry out todays work and then take a little time out. Be still and guard your environment where ever you are. Use the colours that you feel is right for the moment and change if the situation needs it. Next week will show you more clearly what's what. We are always in your midst and we do know how it is.

Blessings and love. TttA

THROUGH STORM AND CALM!

Always remember we are always there in all weathers, and whatever you need or want we are willing to aid you at an instance. Persistence and discipline will get you to your goals. Wait if not given any directions Time is a big factor and you of all people know what it can do. Many times we have seen you wanting to start and being held back. That is a good sign. You have learned patience and are not so hasty. When spirit prompts you is different, act as we advise, all that cleaning up and sorting was very good so keep it as a goal to check and discard all that is no longer needed or wanted. A little more joy is also beneficial, so try to see it from a humorous point. It's always somebody that you can help or give a word to. Stay open for interactions but close off when needed. It's a big plan for you as well as many others. Follow through as much as you are given strength to and spend time with us and enjoy your garden delights. Let's walk together and talk with us in line with nature's spirits.

Blessings as always. TttA

LIFE ETERNAL!

Try a little harder to look at your life as an eternal picture. You then will get a better prospective of your life and where it's all going. Each life time you learn, and love in the best possible way. You can see better when you stand back. Or step outside yourself. All things look clearer from a bird's eye point view. When Earth bound go up to the hill and see all. When you are too close to someone or something the same applies. Don't make any changes or big decisions when tired or too occupied. Stillness and nature will balance your nature and help to make the right decisions. Others will try too often to influence you or just to do what they suggest .Stay very clear of these kinds of people and be detached from their mind and egoistic thought patterns. Next week will help you to see, hear and experience many things. Still remember who you are and what your purpose is. Be in the world but not in it. You are still on a visitors permit to Earth.

Eternal and heavenly blessings. TttA

RENEW AND LISTEN!

Remember to sort out where the information comes from and the motive. Don't get suspicious only look at the facts and see what can be done to your advantage. Let go of too many well-doers and so called know it all's. Don't get too carried away with the earthly tasks. You all live in the world and do and follow the law of the country. Today you have one more lesson to see how far some try to push you and what you should think and do. Let all of that add to your understanding of people. So many are different to you so let them explain where they think they are and if anything needs to be altered, ask us. Don't expect others to act as if they know you very well. They only pick up what you are sending out and they only see what their level of understanding is. Still we say send out love and light to all even your adverse acting people. Do your part and leave the rest to us. Relax and smile and all is well.

All our love blessings and cheer. TttA

EXPOSE THE FAKES!

We have told you so many times how to do that. Late last night you got one more glimpse of how some people operate and why. It was necessary for all to see that they are developed enough. Once was more than clear how the psychical expresses the spiritual and it was quite clear what was going on. We are pleased that you could feel and see so you did not need to see that again. Some speak with the voice of angels others are not yet aware what is taking and using their brain so that appears too busy or they stand back. This will get many on the false track. Very much time and money (energy) will go to waste. It was also a big test for you to see how fast you could spot what was going on. Soon you will have new tools and then and then the ones that got stolen can't be used against you or anyone else. It will come back on the user or in this case misuser. A big lesson for you to guard your wisdom and your tools. Let today be a day of peace, joy and restoration. Still use the colour to aid your work and yourself. We were with you and the protection was given.

Love and light. TttA

ENJOY THE DAY!

Let's work together and enjoy each other's company and all the wisdom given. Today the nature is given you another opportunity to relax and recharge. The warm weather will help you to get more energy. Take the chance just to be and look at all variations of colours and scents. The universal kingdom is so rich and full of treasures. Claim big things and ask for the wealth that you are entitled to. Stay clear of negativity and discords. The influences from so many quarters is also disturbing to many. The more sensitive you are the stronger the protection must be and you are feeling the alterations from all sources. We will see to it that your shield is built up and that you have all you need for your work. Carry on with your different work areas in the best way possible. You are getting more clarity about what's going on and stay clear of people that show disrespect, arrogance and disbeliefs. Your whole system is under review and you know that soon it will be sorted. Try to stay patient a little longer. No one can do anything more to get you out of the way.

Blessings and trust with healing. TttA

CREATIVITY IS ONE MORE CLUE!

To be able to create for yourself and somebody else will give you pleasure and help you to balance your energy. It could be very rewarding and give you a lot of you and to many. Also it will help you to concentrate and keep your thoughts focused. Whatever your talents in you were born with you and you would do well to use and learn from them. There are always lessons to be learned from and you have seen that so many times. Life is so full of incidents and its all for to be practically used for growth. A refreshment time is here so for the best possible solution take advice. Still remember everyone have been born with abilities to serve mankind and the universe. Everything is so well planned and the big picture is unfolding in front of your eyes. Study nature and see what cause and effect operates. The time of healing and understanding ways have been teaching you many things. Nothing is for nothing. Even at times you have to wait for an explanation. People that cross your path have a motive and you will learn from it. Mostly it has given you feelings in a mixed bag. Look what comes with them and where from.

Lots of love and wisdom. TttA

TAKE LIFE AS IT COMES!

It's quite important to take in all the changes and the sudden alterations in your stride. Stay flexible and calm whatever life brings you. It's only there to test you. The big word is balance in all conditions. For many people it's very hard and it feels like all work at times, but there is a reason for that. Perhaps not obvious at first. Stand back and wait until it all shows up. Your present condition is only temporary so stay with good advice. Next week will tell a different story. Wait and watch to be an on looker is very valid for now. All is under review so have faith and know that we are watching after all. Rest and relax as much as you can. In changing times it's harder to keep up the routine. A little longer and all will be revealed. Remember to think a connection to us every day. A few surprises are installed for your day. Trust and love will be given in full measure. Claim big things and big things will come. Remember to always have your spirit in charge of all situations. Beware of situations that look too good to be true. Don't make any hasty decisions for now..

Love, light and loyalty from TttA

LET US DO THE WORK!

Surrender each morning and night because you can't know all that's needed for a good solution. You also can't assume anything at this point just follow through each day as it comes. This time of the year, fresh wind is blowing so let that also refresh your mind, soul and body. Enjoy the small and big news and inputs from us. Don't listen too much to the news media. They are mostly trying to brain wash as many as possible. Big changes are a foot so prepare and rejoice. Don't expect things to get sorted quickly as a few times you will have to leave the timing to us. Eternal time is so different from your Earthly invention. Living in the unseen many times will help you to know what we mean. Yesterday you noticed about timing and it was very well organised. Today's appointment changed as well but it was all for the best, and when you wait the outcome will be better and a little alteration here and there will be O.K. Enjoy today's breeze and the beauty of your garden. We will be with you once again for energy healing and wisdom. Open your heart and mind to receive.

Love and laughter. TttA

WAITING TIME!

Still we say wait soon it will be time to do more work. Last night you felt stronger than before. All company and all present received healing and wisdom. The journey is long and winding many times but your captain is in charge so relax and stay confident that all is well because you can't see what's going on so don't try to investigate what it is just leave it to us. Like we said yesterday let us do the work. The whole universe is in a changeable situation and you on Earth have only a small part to play. Still a small chain one linked to the other will fit in together. The same for your Earthly system, one action will react to what's happening to all others. Whatever you do to others will affect the whole picture. Just carry on as you are and remember we are with you and backing you up. This week will prove to be beneficial after all. Have a day of work and recharging. Go with the flow and don't make any new big plans for now. Your life is unfolding well.

Lots of cheers love and support. TttA

ENJOY!

Prepare to enjoy and make the most of the day. Whatever is meant to be will be and its all for the best. So many times and so many lives have gone past and there is a lot of learning still to come. Let life give you from our rich storehouse and its plenty is there for everyone to enjoy.

The need is great for many and many have lost their trust and faith so the supply is waiting at the depot. No one needs to go without joy and assistance. Mostly the act of asking for help is gone so we don't fill it up for what's needed for each situation. Let us be in charge and leave all complications situations sort out also to us. The energy at this time is so changeable so many sensitive people get a lot of different experiences. Keep things in prospective and don't try to analyse too much today you have seen confusions disruptions and an uneasy atmosphere. The cool and calm input will counteract all adversity. Bless you forever.

Love laughter and joy. TttA

LOVE AND LIGHT!

Let love and light enter your whole being so that you can show others and yourself how the love and light can transform your life by acting as an example you will aid the spreading of human more evolved conditions. As for you, you are being transformed and you will help to transform many others. Stay persistent and look at your goal. Head way is being made to keep going. As you connect and understand more you will remember more from past lives. And use it for many others benefit for all that come. Keep on having trust, faith and clarity about when why and who you will deal with. Always remember to deal with yourself first so the energy can be transferred from us through you to others. You are only a link together with many other light workers to form a chain of input from your teachers in other dimensions. Rest easy and still only take a day at a time. All the last few months have given you a big change. Ponder and give thanks to all input. It's all God's grace.

Remember who you are. TttA

WELCOME YOUR NEW LIFE!

Open up to more input from the source. All this past learning and connecting was for what is starting now. Many times you have been asking about timing, now you are able to see how much it depends on all parties working together and be willing to aid and support each other and the cores of light spreading on your planet. We have now been watching you for years and at last it's bearing fruit. Some people have been very busy disbelieving or being confused about you and what you are. All that is now changing. The true students are getting sorted so the work can carry on faster. You are still human and still have a spiritual quest to fulfil. The higher you go the more time is needed to be spent with us. You have done just that and still have time for all necessities. Today it will be one more day of connection, love and light. The experience you now have will be different from other years. You have served your apprenticeship for a long time. Still do your work and keep on learning every day.

Eternal love and blessings. TttA

LOVE AND LIGHT!

Let love and light enter your whole being so that you can show others and yourself how the love and light can transform your life by acting as an example you will aid the spreading of human more evolved conditions. As for you, you are being transformed and you will help to transform many others. Stay persistent and look at your goal. Head way is being made to keep going. As you connect and understand more you will remember more from past lives. And use it for many others benefit for all that come. Keep on having trust, faith and clarity about when why and who you will deal with. Always remember to deal with yourself first so the energy can be transferred from us through you to others. You are only a link together with many other light workers to form a chain of input from your teachers in other dimensions. Rest easy and still only take a day at a time. All the last few months have given you a big change. Ponder and give thanks to all input. It's all God's grace.

Remember who you are. TttA

WELCOME YOUR NEW LIFE!

Open up to more input from the source. All this past learning and connecting was for what is starting now. Many times you have been asking about timing, now you are able to see how much it depends on all parties working together and be willing to aid and support each other and the cores of light spreading on your planet. We have now been watching you for years and at last it's bearing fruit. Some people have been very busy disbelieving or being confused about you and what you are. All that is now changing. The true students are getting sorted so the work can carry on faster. You are still human and still have a spiritual quest to fulfil. The higher you go the more time is needed to be spent with us. You have done just that and still have time for all necessities. Today it will be one more day of connection, love and light. The experience you now have will be different from other years. You have served your apprenticeship for a long time. Still do your work and keep on learning every day.

Eternal love and blessings. TttA

A NEW DAY!

A fresh change and a fresh start for every day. It's more important to let yesterday go and start again. Many issues have been thought about and so much is changing. Once again you have followed through and tried your best to cope with life and how it has turned out differently and so many lives got involved. Keep on trying your best so you yourselves and others that come in contact with you will feel and benefit from the change. Don't think too much about any outcome for now. It's all in the melting pot once again. What we are doing is to hold the pattern for each individual so we can assist when asked to. The spiritual quest is not so easy. At times you have wondered and pondered why so many different times for different souls. That is because it's a choice and very different for each on their journey towards fulfilment. Each life has its own dialogue and learning to do. As you now understand more we will give you more advanced situations to deal with. Try to see it as we see it. Let each day give you a chance to grow.

Eternal blessings and light. TttA

ANOTHER DAY!

Another chance to work and play and add to your knowledge. Everybody needs to look at their path and journey through life. Once again you have seen and heard from many how their priorities and choices are. Just be an observer and learn from it. So much still to do and you have seen what loveless life does to the physical. It's all connected and as many think you can't heal only one part. It goes through the whole system and when one is suffering the others do it also. Today try to balance all four parts so you can experience so much more. Keep alert and look around you to see how much you have to be grateful for great opportunities to give thanks for all the love, care and support in your life and work. Carry out todays work and rest and relax in between. Say often all is well and in the name of Jesus we will win. Stay grounded and focused to be in balance in all things. Stay close and stay positive is the two words for today.

Lots of love, laughter and life. TttA

RENEW YOUR STRENGTH FROM THE SOURCE!

Stay close to the source more now than before. The closer you are the better the protection, strength and wisdom you get. The chain cannot be broken when the links are solid and dependable so will life be just those for people that come to you. Pass on what we give you and come back to us for more. The storehouse is full and that will stand forever. Today you will hear more about your quest so listen carefully and take in what's valid for you. Many think they have the answer for everyone but it's not so valid. Meaning well is not enough. It's all about the person them self that needs to learn how to self-heal. The healer is only helping to activate the life force so the action can be taken. Remember to ask in the name of the father where all energy, life force and wisdom come from. Keep that picture in mind. When you are doing your part of the work. Let's stay together and have a good clear communication time. You are trained so keep on learning all you can digest.

Eternal blessings. TttA

ORDER!

Try as hard as you can to have spiritual, mental, emotional and psychical order. It's all working together so don't neglect either part. The balance is very beneficial and helpful to your life. When you have surrendered leave it to us to deal with. Of late you have experienced many signs and changes that are because of life it 'self. Don't query too much you have enough to do as it is. The warmer weather will assist you also in feeling alive. The storms that come are more to clear the air and give you more energy. Don't ask too many questions at this point. It's all unfolding as it should. Give yourself power praise and persistence. It's all there to use. Trust and faith will get you through as we often have said to you. Soon you will experience more sights, love and wonders. Keep warm positive and focus on a perfect solution. The strength and sound advice will be given daily. We your team is very close and we will and we do have your growth in your special field in our best interest. Enjoy the rest of the day and smile a bit more. Let your love and light expand.

Eternal blessings TttA

STAY FIRM!

Try not to alter anything after a firm decision has been made. In your case because you are seeing both sides of the situation stand back and let the source give you more input as to what way you should decide to take. You have been tested a lot lately and it has caused you to get stressed out, so now when you have done what was your part wait and listen in. Let no one push you to choose or what's best for others involved. It must come from you and you know what is requested from you for your growth and best interest. Today your view has cleared the path so more decisions can be made. It's not so easy to choose but you are doing your best. We all know how hard it has been. Still we say don't assume anything. Collect all the facts first and then think for a while. Ask us for the right words when talking to someone. The time out today helped you to see all the complex strands of life. Your conditions have been taken care of. Rest in that promise. Stay patient and balanced as much as you can.

Love and light always. TttA

FOLLOW THROUGH!

Yes, we can't say that often enough. Please follow through what's on your agenda and what's needed to be learned. It's all about learning how to handle life and people. Stay close to us and you will feel the force of life and at the same time you will enjoy our knowledge and healing. Take every day as it comes and don't make too many decisions yet. Soon you will see why. Waiting for a cue like some say in the big drama of life. Many people don't see what's going on or why, so tell them. Talk to us first and don't be tempted to rush ahead. Many times impatience could cause a lot of grief. Beware of situations that make you feel uneasy and not relaxed. Look deeper into the motives of every one. Most have not given actions a thought so they just carry as the impulses lead them. Let the day unfold as it may. It's all in the making so stay vigilant and as cheerful as possible. Wait with any alterations inside and out. What is already on its way deal with it. Let's walk together and keep very close.

Blessings for the day and always. TttA

DISCIPLINE!

Let no one put you off or distract your life and work. You are seeing more of that lately. Last night you had a better connection with us and others present did feel that as well. The whole yesterday was a test to see how you would handle many different situations on different levels. That went O.K. but other forces were also taking notice of your progress of spreading the light. More and more cases are coming to your door for spiritual in out. They mostly come for a practical reason but their spirit moves them to talk and want to more of spiritual connection and growth for their own understanding. The light is on so keep it on. The leak is still to be worked on and the student of life will come and be of a good solution. You will hear more today of another spiritual quest. The group will increase in size. Let all that to us we always call the ones that want to come or listen and get healing and up-liftment. Keep your focus and discipline up, it's a part of your training.

Love and light. TttA

SEE THE BEAUTY IN IT ALL!

My beloved children everyone is beautiful. The outer mimic the inner, but too many only see what the first impression is, so stop and get to know who the whole person really is. Life has damaged and many still have weeping sores. Therefore the healing must begin from the inside and that can only be done with love and light from the source channelled down through so many light workers on Earth. You still know who they are by looking at their eyes and what kind of feeling you are getting from them. Study life and what brings life. When you have done your part rest before the next lot comes in. Get a refill and enjoy all that good energy that's freely given. Also we want you to think about life's lessons and why they are so severe for so many. You sure have dealt with cases that requested extra input. Very wise to do your part and ask for the rest to be dealt with from a higher prospective and not been shown the big picture you cannot answer all questions. Enjoy what you can and don't work too hard.

Eternal blessings TttA

LOVE AND LIGHT TO ALL!

We your teachers are all around you and protect guide and heal you when you ask. Don't despair if little hick ups appear or interruptions come. Its only there to test your patience or your knowledge. Keep on applying our lessons for you and your kind. Blessings and light for ever more. Give today of your compassion, love and healing for yourself and the ones that enter your place or connections in the unseen. Be open and receptive listen carefully and follow through. It's only advice and not an order. It's for you to practise and teach others. Count your blessing and smile to show others how much they will add to their journey this time. Enjoy the great time we spend together and be grateful that we can. Your physical is coming right. It's a long road and you are coping just fine. Nothing is wrong only redoing and refining. Carry out todays work and play and all is well with you and the world. Beloved child of light we love you.

Thank you amen. TttA

ASK AND YOU WILL RECEIVE!

Please remember this is so. At times you might have to wait, that is because others involved are not ready. The big –plan is very much up to date, and many situations are already being dealt with. When you ask in honesty we listen and take your request seriously. When you experience other forces you will also have negative input. The slyness of the other ones and the clever disguise is very much seen at present time. Today you will get all the help you ask for. Maybe not the way you know but it still for the best. People and weather is so changeable for a while yet so stay detached and positive. Work as we suggest and take a little more time out. The change will benefit you and enhance your life. Others will try to tell you what, when and how be polite and only take in what you feel is right. Patience for a while longer. It's only temporary what's going on now. Stay as alert and relaxed as possible.

Blessings be upon you. TttA

CLARITY!

Make sure you have all the facts before dealing with situations, and that the environment is clear of all negativity. It takes a lot of time and work to be able to do what's right at this particular time. The discipline of life itself its very necessary to deal with before advancing further. Stay very close to the source and keep on demanding in the name of the father, son, and Holy Spirit. Whatever's good for your higher self? Check and double check. Take your time and don't act in haste. Only if it is an emergency if the spirit prompts you. Back to basics and stay very steady. Be outside if possible every day and relax in the sun. The life-giving rays of my son is very beneficial for all. The nature is waking up and so are you, so go with the flow and enjoy your day as it is presented to you. Rest assured that all is well and your life is coming up to a higher level.

May the goodness of life's blessing come to you. TttA

FOCUS!

Let no one stop you doing your intended work for the source. You are very focused lately and have interested may others of life. Many people have other ideas how everybody else should run their life and especially yours. The idea is to run all investigations on their own life so others could be left alone if not asked. Many use that as an excuse so not any over for their own sort out. The responsibility of each persons to be answerable for their own life if then someone ask for help to listen and then ask us. For the right input for that soul, otherwise you rob that person of their lessons and use a lot of energy of your own for the wrong reason. Empty the feedback today and see it there for a reason and discard all that is doing you any good and give something every day of energy food or wisdom. That will make your day brighter and lighter. Make sure that no stale energy is building up some were. Don't ask for exact timing only a sign or guideline.

Blessings and love. TttA

GET YOUR REFILL FROM NATURE!

Let us send you whatever you need for your work and life through nature. May be flower birds and bumble bees. Whatever tells you about us and the rich universe? The storehouse is full of treasures and all you have to do is ask. When nothing appears wait the timing is not quite right yet. Remember not to get too carried away with anything or anyone. Balance is of most value to all living things. If you get out of that order stop and look at once which area needs to be upgraded in your spirit growth. It's all connected so have another look at what is missing and in what area. Take stock and see, removing to see and revaluate what life brings you. Many will at times be. That is O.K. for now. Waiting time is nearly finished and miracles will appear. Go easy on yourself and beware of leaches in any form and shape. Give out of wisdom love and support every day, we will after requests to refill your vessels. Life is about to open up for so many that have patiently been waiting for the tide to go out to see again.

Eternal blessings. TttA

SING TO THE WORLD!

Let the world know what's inside your soul. Many would like to know where you get your wisdom, love and spirit inputs. Go ahead with today how it comes much is not yet to be revealed. A good solution is on its way and you will be delighted with all the ways it will appear. Many people are already involved in the big picture, so it has been working for a long time. The tests has been many and severe. Let your life and work unfold as it was meant to be. All for the good of your travel through life and its many lessons. Work will come in and other expressions of your work will be noted and exchanged. Put out love and light to all and it will bear fruit many fold. Still we say take a little time out and just to be and watch the bird fly by. The nurturing will also improve. Most people don't really know you as we do so be patient, smile and laugh a little more. You are getting through.

Courage my friend TttA

THE RIGHT TOOL FOR
THE RIGHT WORK!

Let's talk about the tools, as it's only a way to get things activated and help you to focus. Lately tools have disappeared but some will return and others will come in their place when advancement has taken place. Different tools will no longer be useful. Everything goes in a spiral form and are forever evolving. Stagnation is not good for anyone and what are going on now are revelations, orations and anticipation. Today events are revealing themselves as they must. The same again with time is a very important part of the pattern. Stand back and look at what you see is very valid. Being too close to anything or anyone uneasy or more foggy, so before deciding stand back. Get life in to prospective and don't get emotional about anything. It will drain you of energy and distort the picture. Relax and smile for the progress being made. Keep going and don't look back. Stay steady and strong. Enjoy the new form of life.

Blessings and love. TttA

MORE REVELATIONS!

This is the time of revelations. Many are trying to hide or distort your picture about your life. Caution is warranted. Most people that are playing only think they know it all and don't challenge you. You know when they are not telling the truth so send them away with love and light it would be a waste of your time to proceed. You did feel and see before but this last story sharpened your vision. And your confirmation from us told you the story. So many think they are channelling from Christ energy. Many times they have been fooled themselves. Some are quite naïve and believe anything they hear. All technical facts needed to be checked and that will improve your life a lot. Keep on observing and feelings that you get from others that's your way to check. Others have theirs space so leave them to it. Enjoy your day and be grateful that you have such good life as you have. Try to see others point of view as clear as possible, and still keep to yours. Brighter times ahead and many will come only keep the once with positive attitude. And show respect.

Blessings in many forms. TttA

PEACE AND HARMONY!

At all costs remain in our peace and its harmony. No work will be done in my name if confusion, disharmony and unrest are present. Stop at once and let my love and light surround you. Nothing is stronger than that. Trust and don't be afraid. We care for your guardians, helpers and healers. Past trauma is not easy to deal with but you are doing just fine. Believe and trust yourself, you are doing just great. All that not from the light will go and with strength. Courage and joy will be yours forever. Than you can carry out our work and yours in great multitude. Let the day unfold in harmony and hope. We do know how you feel. We are strengthening your field so nothing will ever disturb you again. Keep on working and unwinding for the rest of the day. Say all is well in the name of Jesus how many times that you feel is needed. Blessings and joy forever.

Have courage and work will come. TttA

ANOTHER STEP UP ON THE LADDER!

Progress is being made so keep up the good work. When you look further back you can easy see what was happening. Only by stepping up or aside will you get a clearer view and more insight. Things are unfolding and not the way or time that you thought, but all is working in your time. You know that is divine timing. And the very best for you at your pace. Today one more task will be accomplished. That is what we mean when we say a day at a time. Rather a task at a time. You got extra support and help last night, and we did hear your prayers. A fresh start in many areas will benefit many and your work will increase again. You are getting more insight and much stronger. Let us keep on teaching, healing and guiding all of your past away from many others so called knowledge. Many get the ego in the way and make beliefs too naïve and lacking in judgement as to who is who. It's all a part of development so look at it with compassion, love and light. Carry out what is for today and give thanks to the universe.

Amen to that. TttA

LEAVE THE PLANNING TO US!

Let us guide, heal and give you all the tools that are needed. Beware of souls that are trying to control or advise or make any alterations in your thinking. Don't become fooled or distracted by all the mind operations that are going on. No one can do anything to you if you don't let them. Stay clear of negative entities or situations. Be joyful and spread the good news about the love and light from us. Nothing is as strong as that. Take it all in your stride and keep the courage wisdom and love coming from your heart and soul. Smile in adversity and don't give any energy for them to feed on. Let us deal with that as well. Yesterday was one more clearing job done. It will help your feelings about focus and concentration with peace. Take time in the sun and enjoy the birds and flowers. Still we say be flexible and take only 24 hours in to your plans. Let the day unfold and take notice of speech, actions and vibrations. To be an observer is very beneficial. Blessings and our eternal help healing and wisdom stay with you all.

Your loving team. TttA

A PEACEFUL SOUL GIVES
A PEACEFUL BODY!

One parts feelings will always transfer to other parts. It proves that all are connected and living. Study this truth and use it in your daily life. The inner strength of all living things is also coming from your creator and living friend. The blessing given at birth will give you a fresh start then it's up to you to grow from there. Ignore the wisdom and you will stagnate for a time so stop and remember how much further you would have been if you followed through the information meant especially for you. Every soul is so individual because of every journey through every lifetime to be able to see and practise what is there for you to understand and advance from. Accept what comes it's only a signs that will tell you a story about your life. Join forces is advisable for now. Many of you struggle thinking that they are the only ones that are dealing with conditions. Choose your connections. Check for motives and energy levels. Tonight we will meet again in stillness and recharging with extra input and healing.

Your loving team. TttA

Perspective is good!

Keep your life in perspective means don't underdo or overdo anything, you know situations can change and at times this has caused an energy drain. Keep also in mind that life is never the same for two people. All is similar at times but not in detail. The solution is there for different doses. The sensitive ones get smaller doses but often to be able to digest only a little at a time. Others are able to take it all in at once. Remember when you deal with people check which level they operate from and in which way is best to give the answers. Fine tuning and to be able to see it from where they are at present. It will save any energy drain and a lot of unnecessary time. Learn to go deeper and look at different levels. The main thing is to get through to their spirit and help with whatever is needed. If you are not sure say nothing, just be so you can see the big picture. It's not easy to have your system but it makes you a very good channel. We know about peoples mind games- so do you, stay clear when that's apparent. We are very close now so the solution is coming.

Blessings and love. TttA

EVOKE THE SPIRIT IN YOU!

The Holy Spirit and every one's spirit will one day unite and work together. If we are not accepting the light and wisdom no connection will be made and stagnation will follow. That is what we mean by sorting out time. All of us have to make a stand and a choice. Soon, very soon, you will get proof there are things and situations that are out of your hands and are better left with us. The divine love is different than Earthly love. The divine love will always love you whatever you do and think. The divine love empowers your love. Relax and let go of the unnecessary. When change needs to be done always go to the divine source. Deep eternal love is the very source of life and healing. Pray and claim whatever you want and then the activation will begin. Rest assured that is a promise from the eternal living source. Keep on spreading the word of refilling, regaining and restoring. Peel off the outer layers and go in to the core. Always dig so deep as you want to find your treasures.

Loving light and joy for the day. TttA

SEE WHAT'S THERE!

Let us show the way and point out warnings and observations and give you ideas of what to do next. Your life is so different from many others so it's hard to fit in at times with isolations and withdrawal. That is how it should be you need to take heed and follow through. If nothing occurs that is how it should be. Accept it and wait for the next move. The day will come when it's all sorted. You have for a long time sorted, moved and pondered to find the seed of information, health and rest is indeed a treasure. Never let go it will sustain you throughout your whole life. Abide is an old fashion word but it gives you reassurance and peace. Just be at times is enough and you have experienced all of that. Too much work or not enough is both out of balance. At all times a little at the time so you can fully take advantage of our teachings. And enjoy the time we have together. Enjoy the garden more not only to be worked just be and get all the natural energy from the colours and crystals. The variation of shades of colours will show you the similarity. Keep that in mind when dealing with them.

Glory to God. TttA

LOVE AND LAUGHTER!

Take notice of who brings love and laughter to you. Stay with them and enjoy it, others that bring misery and doom have to go elsewhere. The wants and needs are many for most, so get it all in order accordingly to grades. Don't get drawn in by wolves in sheep's clothing. Many are the ways by the opposition to gain ground closer to you. Go ahead with work today and stay detached and act with compassion. Time will soon go and all is well. You are gaining in wisdom and patience filling your path with grace and joy. These are still waiting times and you are getting close to the end of this chapter. Wait until we give you the OK to move. The many changes that are going on is changing the energy and altering many conditions. Still we say leave it alone and do what's on your plate. All of you have talents so use them for the good of all. Let people do what they want and stay an observer. Life is unfolding so unfold with it.

Courage and love. TttA

STAY CLOSE!

How important it really is to stay close so that you don't put out too much of your path and work. Influences from many quarters are trying their very best to mislead or confuse all that is venerable. If you are not asking about anything don't listen. Ignore as much as you can and keep on working on your assignment. It's have been a very time lately but you have done very well under trying circumstances. The test is quite severe for many souls. Use sun and water to counteract situations and make sure that you are clear from others energy that is not wanted. Your life is about to alter for the better. We know how much you want another level of understanding. Don't listen to doom and gloom, it's only the world's ideas. If you are not comfortable in any one's company, then leave and withdraw. Others have also being tried and attacked so have compassion for all. New souls will come to the group and they will bring new energy in. We are sending them to you so let us keep on doing so when the time is right.

Blessings and all is well. TttA

Calm in the storm!

Let our calm keep you balanced and cheerful at all times. Go ahead and stay as positive as possible. Don't worry too much. Things go strange at times. Just leave it alone and have a rest. Go easy on yourself and others, you are O.K. and will get better and better every day. Keep up the good work and take a day at a time. Tomorrow comes soon enough. The garden will help today and enjoy the warmth and colours that it brings. All the greeneries and plants and the water sounds will give you peace and balance. Nothing can hurt you any more so trust and don't be afraid of the unseen forces. I am stronger than all others so are you. Remember to say that often. To take a deep breath is also helpful. Sit outside today as much as possible. The energy from your garden will help to relax you so enjoy it as much as you can. All is indeed well. Surrender and let us do all that is necessary

Blessings and joy. TttA

TRUST AND FAITH!

Let us two follow you wherever you go. What's important do, and leave the rest for another day. Too much of one thing will make you tired. Ask each morning what is for today and then ask for guidance and tools. So many people have so much talent and are so different in understanding. The result will come out to the end in many different versions for them and their progress. Accept our truth and use it to help others. To see the guiding light for their pathway. No two people stay the same as it might seem at first glance. Dig deeper and behind the mask you will see the situation clearer. Yesterday's input was beneficial for many. As you treat one they will in their turn treat others the same. This is the ripple on the water effect. Be careful what you think more than what you say. The spoken word has power, but the thought is stronger still. Blessings and love for your persistence and courage.

Amen to that. TttA

CALM AND JOYFUL!

In all weathers and all situations stay calm and smile. You have been tested in all areas to see how you deal with it. Again and again you have gain victory. It has taken a lot of time and energy with understanding for you, that is O K. Time is only man made anyway so its only something that humans use to have a timeslot. To be practical is good but don't neglect other parts. You will find out more and more how it really works. Go on with your work and rest today. Take a little time out in the afternoon and just be. Your life is still improving and you will enjoy more variation in life. Technical things are tricky at times but you will conquer. Always listen and trust me. I am with you all the time and encourage and love you for your trying, teaching and healing in my name. Time has gone but concern yourself about age and don't ever limit yourself. You are advancing and learning. Keep up the persistence and love and laugh.

From your ever loving team. TttA

CELEBRATE!

Today we like you to have a look at how much you have to be grateful for and celebrate the way you are cared for and uplifted so many times. We know that you have free will still we say how to learn and exist. You can always ask if in doubt and what to do and when. You can always leave it alone. Give away something every day. That makes the energy turned over and plenty will be returned to you. It could be spiritual mental, emotional or physical. Whatever is appropriate at the time. Feel what is right and then act upon that. If uneasy in your guts (3rd chakra) then don't. Many times all are tested and tried so we are making sure that you can do more advanced work. It's all in stages and degrees so you can easy grow and accept lessons. Still do your homework and spend time with us every day. Let nothing disturb you or block you in any way. Thus days are gone. Today is a fresh start and once again you have learn to wait. The same goes for relationships and connections. When we say wait you would be wise to do so.

Have a day of peace joy and music. TttA

SUNSHINE AND ROSES!

Enjoy the nature and scents that it brings. Recognise the beauty in all living things. Let us care and protect you. We know best about your combination. You are learning every day, so you are getting better every day. It's a long way to go yet all you can do is follow through, day by day. Concern about tomorrow will take the joy away from today. Plan a little and keep up your regime. It's only for a while longer and you have been very patient and have made many wise decisions. Not all but as long as you are working on your path it's O.K. It's all to do with progress, patience and persistence. Keep life as simple as possible, less things to sort out later. Only go with your spirit flow not the flow of the world. Separate and still be practical about life. All connections of yours are getting sorted, so leave them to us. You have done more than your share. Today will be interesting and revealing. Remember always to have spirit in charge.

Love and light. TttA

OPEN YOUR HEART!

Open up and shut doors and welcome new situations to come in to you. For a long time you have been teaching and wondering how when and who. That is understandable to get your balance back in your life. In your case we know you better than everybody so a good solution for you is coming. In springtime new life is coming from the creator and so also to you. A long time has passed more than usual but for a good reason. It seems that you will know soon and be glad that all is working and in good condition. The new order in your life will be very beneficial for yourself and very many others. Keep on having discipline and try to keep an open mind about people and events. The long-time of detachment and seclusion for your recovery and recharge. Still beware of motives and side tracks. Spend time outside when possible and get more energy from the garden, pets and colour. You will succeed and blossom once again. Thank you for your input of spirit and progress. Today is a part of the new beginning. Bless you.

Eternal love. TttA

RESPECT EACH OTHER!

To show respect and listen in to what other people say or want is good. Sometimes you don't hear it all. What is not said is often the most important Talk to their spirit and then you will have the correct answer. Many spirits are so downhearted and tired so nothing gets said or done. Go ahead with your plans and don't be disturbed by too much talk and interference. Silence is often the big healer. Too much is going in a very short time so wait until we give you the OK. Beware of too much talk at this point. All need a time to just be. Just wait and let other people come to you. Don't give advice if you are not asked. But In an emergency from us, do tell and pass on the advice. Breathe in slowly and be outside today. Not long now and you can enjoy peace and quiet. Today will bring you some news and you soon will feel more at ease. Your system is so sensitive to others feelings and vibrations that you have a physical reaction. Nothing is wrong only at times you wonder what's going on. Ask us and we will strengthen you. Let today be a day of serenity and joy.

Blessings and peace. TttA

STAY WITH THE KNOWLEDGE!

To be able to stay and develop with the source is indeed a privilege. Today you have seen a little interference and you know what it was in a second. Keep on trying to identify what's what so you can see the pattern. The last few days you have experienced different motives and a lot of confusions. Tonight you are aware more so be an observer and understand that the ones that come were sent by us. You are keeping your promise and so are we. The lovely garden is doing a lot for so many. You have come to a higher understanding so that you can see much better. It's no use to fog you in so it's not working so it will make your days easier. Stay positive and anything that you need for your higher self is yours. No need to struggle and exhaust yourself. Rest when tired and shut your door when needing solitude. Confusion in many cause them to see a distorted picture. Some are very convincing but will not succeed. Stand your ground and enjoy the surprises. Things are on the move so even you don't see it, it's going on.

Courage and peace. TttA

STAY FIRM AND CALM!

Nearly this race has run. You then will have a new race on a higher level for the source. Don't think for a moment that you are finished only another chapter in your book of life and many more to come. Get ready and don't listen to doom and gloom. Too many others are doing just that. To get carried away is one thing so look at what you are carried away by. Always look at your leaders before you do any major changes in your life. Your type of work is different so understand that your life's experiences are also different. Expect good things to happen and they will. Negativity is the thing that anyone grows from so let the day unfold as it may. Don't plan too much as the natural ways is best. Big change in your life is instore. Reward for your work and persistently done. Just a short time and you are doing the right thing and all is well. This months out and you will see. Settle down and listen to your music. The attack will stop and you will have peace. Trust and don't be afraid. Amen to the glory of God.

Courage from us. TttA

RENEW!

Recycle some, exchange or discard others that no longer serve your purpose. Others might want to have some or give away what's not needed. That will give you a fresh feeling of waiting for something to fill in the empty spaces. Different stages, different needs and wants. The same goes for food colours and contacts. All is there at certain times to teach observe and learn from. Let today be a day of sorting, growing and taking advice from the source. Wipe your slate clean then start again. What's gone has to be gone. Living on past situations and grief does not do anything for attracting other searching souls. Today will also bring news about a long standing query. All is getting sorted as we have said so many times. Surrender and only do your part as we advise you. The warmer days are now here so enjoy the life giving sun. Watch the garden come alive and get invigorated by colours and nature In these changeable times. You need to spend more time apart and close to the source.

Blessings be upon you. TttA

KEEP ON RECHARGING!

Let this waiting time be used to recharge before all that battle and strife begins. Because you are under my protection the onslaught will not be so severe. All the ones that you work with will have the same privilege also. The tension you are experiencing is a sign that you know about mind control and brain washing so stay apart from all that. The work that it brings could make you feel separate but that's the idea, to go in to your safe haven and feel secure. Many years of hard work has made you little tired and the need for positive input and all that clearing and cleaning is going on also help to take energy. Rest assured that you will not perish lets walk and walk together. Your new hobby is very beneficial for you and using the colours of nature will also aid the healing process. You deserve the very best and you have asked many times what now and which way. The end result was that as long as you pray with a pure heart we will give to you what's beneficial for you. Some students think that all the work done is of benefit. Every thought of love and light is very valid.

Blessings and thoughts to all. TttA

SEE THE BEAUTY IN ALL!

Let's look at the beauty and love in all living things. Many don't show it or let anyone discover it because of lives experiences or fear of others opinions. Open up to the inner beauty and focus on that love and light from the source that we bring into very searching souls. You have a saying on your planet that says beauty is in the eye of the beholder. Scars and imperfections will not be noticed when love is there so in each case call in your team and try to understand how to open up this door. It will be hard for a perfectionist to see a lot of beauty in many. We say go past the author and see what we see, like a crystal that has been buried in the Earth and come to light and was washed in the river of light. After you will enjoy the sparkle of all the facets and get a glimpse of eternity. So much beauty is not getting recognised or appreciated. Too many sad and broken hearts will then exist again. Go on with an expression today of colour, sound and love. Study lines and volumes and take notice of what grows or what does not.

Blessings and peace. TttA

TRUE LIGHT AND INFINITE LOVE!

My children of Earth we want to remind you about light and love. Thus two are the main ingredients in the universal teachings. You have heard so many times about it so you know nothing can be done without that. Many have tried using many other ways but that's not working in such a powerful way. All of you get side tracked now and then. That is not wrong; it only delays your goal which is in sight. Lessons could also be learned and situations might be clarified if you did not get side tracked. Nothing is for nothing and you have wondered many times about that. It's always one more way that could help and explain to you. Don't act before you are absolutely clear. Too many people that act in haste have to go back and redo some situations. The exception is when spirit talks to you and it's an emergency. Today is a day for getting organised and express yourself in a creative way. Some changes of energy are about so use them for your life and enjoy what comes your way. Blessings with love and light for all that is living and working for the good of all mankind.

Support and health from all of us. TttA

ORDER!

Keep order and get things done. One thing at a time will get you through the workload. Keep in mind that all things need maintenance. The first thing you have to do is maintain your soul development then all others will be done as well. Relax and smile and all is indeed well. Many in your world are doing their best to rattle you at any cost. They will eventually give up so you then have conquered your lessons. Let the day unfold as much as it should. Now is the time for looking at what you want and give some away that are no longer useful to you. Refresh and restore to a better situation than before. Enjoy the little surprises and still we say be flexible and let us be in charge. Don't concern yourself about situations that are out of your control. You did ask us when you surrendered so let us deal with them. We will tell you about signs and omens so you can get back to us more often. This time you must try to grasp the big picture. Don't get influenced by others that are supposed to know the truth. Keep your strength and courage up.

From your loving team. TttA

STAY FOCUSED AND CALM!

Many times at present there is a lot of misinformation and confusion. Stay clear of all of that you are not there to get involved in. Their worlds matter. Your task is to get a link between the dimensions and to do bridgework. The connections are at many times different because of the spirit levels. You already know that is needed so try to explain the simplest way possible and go ahead with your plans. We have given you all your tools and when you require more just ask and it will be given in an instant. Many times you nearly have given up but we know you will run the whole race all the way. Do have a pause when tired and then listen in and then empty out first so you will keep a steady stream of energy coming down and never ever go short of what's actually needed. Relax and enjoy the input from us tonight. We do know how much work is being done by so many light workers down on Earth. The angels are also in close contact daily with you to heal, teach and support you in your daily work for the source. You are learning, growing and grasping the truth.

Amen and thanks. TttA

Cheer and care!

Many times you wonder why and that is understandable. Many things are appearing and there is a strong energy about today. Many try to ignore and don't respect. That is not the right [picture of you. Well that is their own responsibility and leave them to it. Recharge and relax today. You are on your way slowly but surely. Many situations are being looked at and a few revelations are coming out. Music and colour will help today and positive thoughts. All is indeed well and carry out a few small tasks. Don't ask too much of yourself and be aware of on hangers. You will conquer and reach your goals. Ask if you feel it's needed. Do what comes naturally today. Wait when we say wait. Wonders are unfolding and you will succeed. Angels and teachers are standing by. Surrender and leave it to us. The big picture is unfolding and many will see the truth. Smile to the faces of evil. They only want energy. Exposed souls are showing up.

Courage and love. TttA

ENJOY THE MUSIC!

It's a blessing to be able to relax and sing. For many is also an enjoyment with the vibrations that come from heaven. You have used sound healing for a long time so keep on doing that. Also your bells and chimes will do the changing in the surroundings. Because of your sensitivity you pick up too much from the environment and from some people. Guard against that and strengthen your field against negativity. This time of the year be outside and listen to nature. In the stillness you will feel peace and restore back to full strength. Ask us for more ideas how and when. Steady does it you are not in favour of noise unease and negativity. We will protect you from all that so you can get on with life. The days are unfolding very fast so we know how it affect you. Keep busy but not too busy. Stop a while and just be. Good advice is very trustworthy and useful. Keep writing and other words going as you are. Lots of peace, love and beauty will come your way. Beware of interference. Learn from it and it will be less.

Blessings and love. TttA

ETERNAL LOVE AND BLESSINGS!

Let us give from our storehouse that is so overflowing and always ready to open the doors when a request is activated. Go ahead with all other things that will help and uplift you. The mountains are for your strength and they will give you a better view. The bird's eye view is always clearer and less foggy. Too close to a situation and you will find it's hard to see what's needed and therefore it will take more effort to untangle a picture. Today you have experienced a new way of looking at certain areas. The paintings will express your feelings and also help you to unwind. Give yourself credit and love yourself as much as you can. Don't wait for someone else to do what you want in 4 areas. Ask us and we will reinforce your energy level. And help you to take a day at a time. Life is unfolding and you are with it. Too many tasks at present and you will find it will recede as you grasp the truth better. Years of learning and study has made you the person you are. We do know about power struggle and how many want to have a piece of the cake.

Blessings and love. TttA

DISCIPLINE!

Order in my kingdom and order in your lives. Let every day have enough of its own and leave all that in the past to us. The future you have not seen yet. That is for us to sort out and then you still have a free will to be able to make a choice that will benefit your higher self is not always easy. Events or situations are very much trying to interrupt whatever is going on. It's a test for you as well as everyone else. All of you would perhaps to have another look at what's lacking and which area. Go back and look what was going on and why. Today is another day so make it new as much as possible, be outside and enjoy the warmer weather. Do what feels normal. Claim peace, joy and health and all will come. Invite the Christ to dwell inside you and he will. Give to him what you cannot understand or handle. The angels are also working for the ones that cooperate. First of all relax and smile, show others what peace and joy from heaven is. Rest assured that all is indeed well.

Loving thoughts from all of us. TttA

LET THE MUSIC SOOTH YOUR SOUL!

Go along today to enjoy the sound of music and feel the benefit of all the different vibrations. Healing with music has long been the one affect most people and you of all now have seen what it can do. Different speeds and combinations are for you to alter for whatever needs to be done. Tools are fine as they are but the one that holds on to the strings from the energy source is shown fast. You all will feel and know when to do what. Tune in and use it as a start every day. Some souls prefer silence and that's good.

Also Inspiration comes from different places of nature. If you are feeling drained look to where the energy is going and who looks recharged. In that case withdraw and come to us. Use colour and get a response inside you of what's doing that to different people. Let go of outside input for now. We have a plan in mind for you so let us do what's needed. Do trust that all is well and are staying so. Calm joy and peace is yours whenever you need or want it.

Courage and blessings. TttA

INTERNAL BLESSINGS!

Let my peace reign in your hearts. So much more will be done and so much more achieved when the preparations have been done. The same as you might know about paintings is only as good as the groundwork. Is that clearly understood? Today you are getting more of your treasures returned. Spirit did borrow them for a specific purpose and you claimed them back. The search was not in vein. It was to do with your trust and beliefs in the source. It's hard for you at times to believe 100 % because of your life and how it has been. No more, you are winning and coming to a new understanding about the universe. It's been a long time well worth the effort. Many would have left the race by now but surrendering and leaving things to us when it's past your knowledge is a wonderful thing. It's safe for you know how to be powerful as long as you remember where your strength coming from. Always keep in mind why you are here and what you have to learn. Stay outside as much as possible to get back what was lacking before. Spread joy and love today, love all and listen in.

Thank you from all of us. TttA

CATCH UP TIME!

Let us be a part of the pattern of your new life. Many arias has been looked at and sorted. Last few days you have seen more of disguises than before. Some people are not aware that you can see what's going on. So they play a little game. The warm sun and th3 fresh air will revive you. Nature is a very good healer and take it as it comes and you will see wonders unfold. The soul yesterday was in need of answers in some areas so he came for more than the work in a way that was beneficial him and his beliefs. It's always more than one way that visit and work skill. That will only be one way they wanted to know and why your intuition is getting very much more improved and your life is also changing for the better. Patience and determination has got you so far and of course we have been backing you up all the way. Keep on taking charge and all situations will be different. Rest in our company and enjoy something every day. Balance your life as much as possible and give thanks for all the goodness.

Calm, joy and peace to all. TttA

CARRY ON!

So much work and so little time before the big change. Hold on and stay steadfast and all is well. Many have asked questions about the big change, well it's not quite ready yet. We are doing as much as we are able, so be patient, you do know and you do know what you are taking about. Many think different but that's O.K. it is nothing to do with you. You are walking on your path and are travelling along on your special journey. That is how it should be. A few minor obstacles underway will not hinder you, only take more time so leave it to us. Relax and be outside when possible. Nature is a very good restorer. We do feel for you but it will not be long now before you can see the fruit and do some harvesting. Many don't understand you and what you are doing so much work. That's not for them to try to explain. You are on a different level so the rules are different. Tools will be returned to you soon. It has been a very severe testing time for many of you. Hold on and keep working.

Blessings and love TttA

Unfolding time!

Let the truth unfold and be looked at in a simple way it all is when you understand what the growth is all about and how you can use it from the source. Love and light is still very important to all so when you have done your homework all parts of you will benefit. When you have learned the biggest part how to unfold in your own speed, it all will turn out right. No use to skip a class ready before time have a pause and recharge, because of all different levels of knowledge backgrounds and circumstances today. It might look like hard work that's right but don't do everything on your own. The struggle and isolation will make you tired, and that is no good for light work. Spread the load of work and then stand back and see what's done and get a bird's eye view of life whenever possible. Enjoy a little break every day, as you can't be expected to run on empty. It all comes back to balance and being the person you are. You have seen it all too often what it will do to a person, and it will also stop the growth in spirit. First see to the source and connect with us. The pipeline has to be clear and unclogged at all times.

Blessings and growth. TttA

Sunshine and roses!

Let the universal love and light enhance your lives. Stop any negative thoughts or actions at once. When in doubt of what to do ask us and you will get the answers. Remember the positive teachers they teach and advise the negative tempt and control. When a situation arises see that the action and the words fit in and then you can act on it. A new way for some but when looking back you can see where you went wrong, and learn from it. Whenever you don't see the situation for what it is you will have another chance to learn in a different way, so open your eyes and ears to the truth and stay captain of your ship. We your teachers are still there but you must learn to make decisions that are wise. What is right for one person is not necessary the same for all. It is very individual for each searching soul. We give you situations that you will learn from then you can go on to next lesson. Have faith and stay calm at all costs as Energy drainage will at times occur. Beware of uneasy feelings and people, they only want a free meal.

Blessings and love. TttA

HEAL AND RESTORE!

Restore to a better condition work and renewal. You all are aware of many changes and you have known that for a long time. Keep on altering what's needed for your work and for yourself. To grow and follow your path is the best you can do, so always remember where your strength comes from and always give back in the end of the day what you can't do including situations, people and Earthly conditions. Many will be opposed to the way of your thinking that is their business. Let the day unfold as it may your life is about to change. More important work for the light will soon show itself. You have now been prepared for some time. All your spiritual mental, psychical and emotional levels have been looked at and they are being restored. New information is being revealed to you and more connections are coming. Still beware of someone that pretend to know and only have a surface idea. Talk to the right channel and relax in between you are on the right track and staying on it will be easy from now and on.

Blessings and joy. TttA

STAY UNRUFFLED IN ALL WEATHER!

To bend and not to break in all disturbances is not always easy. You are working on just that now and it's better and stronger. That's all a big lesson and the story is not over yet. Connections with others similar are essential. Stop afterwards and relax and rest. Even when you feel everything is fine, still we say check. Many spirits come and go so the station of yours is a very good anchor for the light. It's important that you remember that. Some get drawn to the light like moths to a flame. Some only come to sit and recharge for a while. Many souls have different purposes and the same is what the weather does for plants. Like parables you can easy remember the picture we give you. Lessons learned from them give you guidance and light on your journey through life. To be able to see and hear is most valuable. At present time so much is going on and so many need assistance. Remember to sip your water all in the right order and then you will feel the benefit also bless your food and say thank you after. See you tonight.

Blessings and love. TttA

GLORY TO GOD!

Let your thoughts and actions be of glory to God. We, your maker and keeper of all good also let the life force from God enter your spirit with body and emotions. Remember to ask for it to stay there and do what it was meant to do. We are in charge and what everyone thinks that still stands. All have free will and most decide the course of actions. Follow through and listen in you are busy with earthly tasks it would be advisable to spend more time with spirit. And get the input that's needed. So much for all on the planet. All conditions on earth are a sign of pollution, toxins or manmade or negative thinking pattern. Smile and think happy thoughts have faith and keep calm. Breathing pattern is also to be kept in mind at all costs. The new way to sip the water slowly is also beneficial for you and many others. Keep positive people around you and take a little time out.

Cheerful blessings. TttA

LET MY PEACE COME IN TO YOUR HEART!

Nothing valuable can be done for the source if not peace reign in your hearts and the whole being. So much has gone and so much to do. At times you feel like panic, don't! Sit for a while and breathe fresh air or have a little nap and when fully restored start a fresh. Start a fresh and you are progressing day by day. Don't look at one accident and despair, you are going to conquer. Be patient with your body and mind, it will take a little time but you have plenty of that. Sipping water will also help and think positive thoughts throughout the day. All of this dimensions unease is not for you, so that way you are staying clear of the world for now. Many work differently but that's for them. Stay outside whenever possible and keep on doing as best as you can. We know how hard it has been but that was a part of your lessons. Accept what comes and see what there is to see. You want to see what is coming after the New Year. Don't listen to other's woe or conditions as it can be too much. Later you will have a stronger field so understand this time it is so.

Blessings and peace. TttA

IN THE STILLNESS YOU GOT INPUT FROM US!

Let the nature and the peace in your garden give you what you want for the day. The bigger the unease the more withdrawal you have to do. Always look at the source as a way to restore and make it your home. A heavenly home is the most secure and it is filled with treasures and supplies for whatever you need for your work and the environment. Never think that you not have enough of energy, time and tools. All is taken care of and because of your work we are standing by very closely. Let today be a day of beauty, joy and wisdom. Take care to listen in and empty out. The time first thing in the morning is more valuable than you know. It strengthens the bonds and keeps you safe and your mind, and spirit in a receiving frame of mind. The link is also important for us to have a trust worthy light on Earth together with others well trained. Today is a new day so treat is as such. Yesterday is gone and you did learn from it. The new regime will get you settled and tested when called for. Small miracles will occur once again. You will have signs and situations sorted.

Love and light. TttA

COOPERATION!

Please understand by having a good communication and cooperation you will cooperate in a very professional manner. Look again what methods you are using and whom you deal with. Many think they have the answers and some have part of it and many others just want to be heard. The human nature is so in need of focus and attention. Many feel forgotten or misunderstood. The dimension that you are living in is so different from the one that you are visiting at night with us. The difference is great and that's why you feel so different from many others. Your healing session last night was very powerful and the ones that were involved and took notice benefited from it. The human love alone does not sustain it all and it must be accompanied with divine love. It will open your heart to feel the combination of the two together. That love combination will spread out and give others what has been missing in their lives. Divine love always stays the same and whatever you do it's there for you to become in tune with the universe and coming alive with all that wonderful energy.

Blessings for today and always. TttA

ENJOY THE NATURE!

Stay clear of situations that are too busy and minds that are too occupied. All that you work for spirit should try to balance the energy and make sure that you are not doing too much. The need is great and many are ready to look anywhere for a solution. Ask us when and how you should listen or speak. Let tonight show you what spiritual joy and wisdom can do. We will be present and don't concern yourself with its or buts. That is not for you anymore. The big clean up in your surroundings has broken the pattern and also given you more peace and energy. It could not have been avoided it was a part of the pattern that was formed so many years ago. Now it's clear and you can get on with life. Let life flow as much as possible. Withdrawal when needed and get balance back in your life. The last month of the year has begun so a tidy up of conditions is here. Patience and focus is still improving. So keep it up. Let go of well-meaning advice. Psychic is not always spiritual work but a balance between the two.

Cheers and health from TttA

REJOICE!

Rejoice for every little thing that improving and let the days unfold as they may. The future is not there for you to see only every 24 hours as you awaken deal with that, and not other people's timing or order. To be able to listen and stand by is what we often do, ready to assist you and give you advice. Listen to our wisdom and take on board good sound advice. Not many these days are aware of the most important values of old the memories of another era has been forgotten or not used any more. Good habits and positive thinking is very necessary now. Stand tall and fight for yourself and others. That is not your wisdom and teaching but you are a light keeper on your planet. The symbol of a circle is also a sign of togetherness and completion. That is one more reason why you shifted to New Zealand to complete another circle. Most of your part in the work is not recognised. But we see it and that's all that counts. Your new regime has also helped to improve your conditions. Soon it will be better still. Harvest time and much joy.

Eternal blessings and love. Ttta

START AGAIN!

Let no one or any event hinder your progress and disturb you from doing your life purpose. You are strongly and effectively protected so you can do all that is necessary for your part of the cleaning, teaching and healing. It's a new day so all are recharged and done to perfection. The weather is also a part of making your life so much easier. Bright and shiny energies come out from your home and that is why at times get spirit leeches hanging around. Don't do the cleaning work yourself only ask us to deal with it at once. Rest and recharge for every day that's going on and you are improving. More supporters will be entering your group and more will get access to the truth from us though you. Carry out todays work and then take a little time out. Be still and guard your environment where ever you are. Use the colours that you feel are right for the moment. Change if the situation needs it. Next week will show you more clearly what's what. We are always in your midst and we do know how it is.

Blessings and love. TttA

GREEN PASTURE!

Let the colour of green show you what it can do. Colour therapy is used by many to balance what's been out for a while. Relax and visualise the richness of colour. Use what colour comes to mind every day. You may be surprised just how much is activated and balanced. When you get the same colour advice more often than others look in to your lives more closely. The repeat of the same indicates more healing and time out needs to be spent on that specific area. Then you can go to the other part. Gold is another very useful colour solid and steady also genuine. People that can see auras also can tell about colours. Use the basic system to recognise what's going on and what to do. Healing sounds can also improve many situations. The same when you listen to nature that wind, birdsong, waves and an insect brings you. Natural is best and study and listen how it sounds. Communication from living nature could prove very beneficial. Practise a little more to get closer to the life force of other living things. The creator has made it for benefit for all mankind. Enjoy and learn from the creator's expressions of the universe.

Blessings and love, calm and joy extra for today!
TttA

FRESH START!

Let the morning dew revive you and help you to start again. So much is happening in a very short time. Time out was necessary for you. The afternoon time for healing and recharge is a very good idea. Today is a very good day and you will get a chance to catch up and do something that requires peace and silence. The weather is also coming in to a warmer season so you can enjoy more time in the garden. The singing is also beneficial for you and your music clearly with rest will get you in the right frame of mind. This is a season for many to get stressed out or do same silly things. Let it all pass you by. We will be with you most of the time until New Year and then it will change again. You will be more aware and stronger. Until then stay close as all is indeed well. A little work every day and all will be done that's needed. Well the day let it all unfold as it may.

Blessings and love. TttA

Feedback from the source!

Listen in and follow through. That is a part of your lessons. Yesterday you finally you got an answer about your system. That was good and now you can go ahead as planned, uninterrupted. The progress of your journey is going just fine. Patience and trust is playing a very big part of it and you are really going ahead. A long time has passed and you have been wondering, but it was the best way possible for you. We also are reminding you about different dosages for different systems. It needs to be applied individually. And don't take someone else's medicine. You all are so specific in your requirements so ask us and so many situations will be avoided. The more sensitive system you have the more careful you should be. Enjoy the preparations for the seasons as we will be with you most of the time. So all is taken care of. At times you wonder when and what way, leave all that to us. Some of your queries are also too soon to answer we will not forget all in its all good time. Relax and smile a little more.

Lots of love and light. TttA

ONE MORE MIRACLE!

Believe miracles and they will happen. The trust and faith are the two main ingredients to a strong spirit life. Try to see a little more and experience more solutions to an old way of thinking. The last pieces of old ways are going very fast. Out with the old year! Let us encourage and give you cheer. We are the only ones that know your circumstances and all the trial and tribulations you are going through. It will all be sorted as from yesterday you got some more strength back. Too much not going out to too many areas as you have discovered, everyone needs time to recharge. As you have been through a major over haul it has taken a lot of energy to deal with. The worst is now over and you can look forward to a peaceful holyday. Keep on going by your gut feelings and don't be taken in by some that think they know you. Thank you for letting us inform you and for doing your part of the work in proportion today. More tomorrow and cheer up.

Lots of love and laughter. TttA

JOY TO THE WORLD!

Spread joy into a sad and hungry world. The darkness has gone in to so many hearts and minds. It's a sign of the time but not for much longer. It is noticed all over the world and your planet is in for a big shake up you must decide now for to stay undecided at the moment is not benefitting anybody. The planet will be dealt with in time. All will help to stabilize, clean and clear the earth. We are still keeping an eye out about the progress. The battle is still going on. Today is a 5 planet line up so you feel it more strongly than others. Take care and relax whatever comes your way. You are still preparing for a new workload. So gather strength and grow in wisdom, spirit and youth. Late night's unease was caused by the energy shift. It will settle down in time and sooner than you think. Thank you for keeping up the work and the willing ness to energy time and commitment for the good of all mankind.

Blessings and extra love for today from all of us through me your old friend.

TttA

DIVINE TIMING!

Let us explain a little more about divine timing. You, living on Earth are so used to your timeslots and calendars. Stop for a moment and think about it another way. The work that's needed to be done is made so that all pieces fit together and the blueprint is right, so the architect (Me) is in charge. Free will still exists but in spiritual matters you have to understand that that is a sensitive area for many. Divulge an input from spirit so the brain takes over and the result will be so much out of growth and truth. Remind your fellow that the brain is fine but the spirit must be in charge. The subtle expressions of the brain are at times misleading so you might believe that the spirit is in charge. We know how easy that can happen and when not developed correctly, easier still. Love your spirit and mind still the same. All parts of your body are still practical and are needed for the whole picture, just like you do when turning over a picture so you can see the other side better. Understand that truth and you are on your way. Colour is still very important and remember to unwind after each task.

Blessings for the season of joy. TttA

SOLUTIONS FROM THE UNIVERSE!

To be able to see where your answers and solutions are coming from is indeed to be able to have the facts in a very good way. You have seen that much lately so you have had some more proof. To be able to is quite often a valuable thing. Many people just assume what's going on and that can bring on the wrong actions. Be an observer and stand by. Don't do anything if not asked. To be able to see and not do is hard at times, because you can see what's going on, still we say wait. You need your energy for your work and to prepare for the next chapter with much more being accomplished and more will be done. You are being trained for your part with the new life on Earth. Concentrate on your part and others should do the same, and much more will be achieved. Day by day a little clearer and more organised. Remember to be a good listener. Many only give only half ear to another's wants and needs of help. Stay committed and we will do the rest.

Eternal blessings and joy, health, wisdom and youth from us all. TttA

NEWS FROM THE STATION!

All in good time. Only a little every day for you to digest each day. You have seen what too much in one day will do, so balance out all the work. This season is also helping to push things along and same only think of giving others only of receiving. To be one sided is never a good thing so give out as your spirit needs you a lot of peace joy and light. The weather is also changing many storms floods and it's a sign that the Earth needs cleaning up and energy change is taking place. Watch and wait, you are doing your part in your area. Every day is another chance to change what's not in working order. It will also alter the energy levels around when you do. Still send out extra love and light to all as you do it will return in time. Don't make too many plans as yet. The picture is unfolding. Rest assured that all is well and all is as it should be. All tools will be returned to you. More tomorrow.

Blessed be. TttA

GIVE MORE LIGHT AND LOVE TO THE WORLD!

The planet needs to be warmed up and come alive. We have sent a lot of clearing and cleaning methods down so plenty has been done. Keep on sending out more care and compassion and Christmas cheer to all. Many don't let on or ask for help. That is because of early preprograming, too harsh or critical, even when you try your best to reach them with a thought of light and love from the source. Eternal love is so much stronger eternal and always supplying all needs not always what you might think but what is best for your higher self. Look at the motives of gifts and smiles whatever turns up. It's a lesson for you all. Give more of your time, love and listening ear. Leave things how they are at the moment for that day but look a little deeper for more lasting lessons through gifts from spirit that lives in your heart. Keep on doing what you are. Time will soon go and a new year will come with new energy, joy and work in many different areas. Keep the balance and let us know what you don't know how when or what to do. Let people come to you. We give them the thoughts. It's all in cooperation with all together.

Joy, blessings and protection from us all. TttA

PEACE TO ALL.

Let our peace be seen in all souls also pass on peaceful thoughts and actions. Whatever you think and do will multiply so be careful about your thoughts. Your part is to sending love and light, healing, teaching and activating. As a reliable channel you are doing more than your part. This holyday will be cheerful and surprising. Many have thoughts are coming but we are not ready. Now they will make an effort all in the right time and place. We enjoyed to be with you last night for genuine growth must come from the inside and spread outwards. Forgive the ones that interfere or are trying to control. Send them love and light so the change can take place. It's not up to you. Your part is to bridge the gaps and let them meet half way. Thank you for giving thanks to us all. It is a good way to operate.

Blessings for the strength and wellbeing. TttA

THE LIVING SON AND MY SUN!

Blessings for the whole season and rich light and love

to all from the holy kingdom and we always know how the Earth is and we are working towards a united universe. It's been a very long time coming but now it's finally on its way. So many solar system are involved and many wars has been fought among the different beliefs ideas and powers. So many powers except mine, so it is futile to think about wars or any conflicts. So much waste, pain and suffering, all for nothing. Come to me first and then all is well. Egos come in to it often from people that are being ignored. Humans are so bewildered or outcast in one form or the other. To want to be heard is all ego only do your part and we will do the rest. Humans are still not thinking individual has been lost many times. Always stay free of negative or feelings of doubt. We are the only ones that know the full picture, and then again we only have promised once again every 24hours to let you know what's for today. Rest in our midst and keep going as you are.

Go upwards a step at the time, progress is being made. TttA

BLESSED BE!

Let the blessings of the season enhance and make you feel warm and blessed. To be able to refill from the source is your life line so keep the ropes of connection strong and in good order. When the strand in the ropes wears thin the whole thing is less strong so replace the ones that are weak to make it whole again. Watch and stay vigilant as things are on the move so be focused and patient for yourself and others. Daily steps and progress is being made. The journey is long and winding. Many times you wonder how much more to learn but that's not for you to decide it's for us. Keep on learning and loving and light a light every day so you are acting as a light house on Earth For mankind. Be grateful for what you have and give thanks for all things even if you don't understand why. It's all in the plan of your life unfolding. Ask for more clear guidance and a way to check who is who. Keep your actions and thoughts positive and give uplifting love and light to all you connect with this season. You are indeed a messenger from the creator.

Love and light. TttA

INSPIRATIONS!

Look at where are you getting your inspirations from. The action of each person is telling a story. Study and find out. You will soon see and that will help you and know what to do much sooner. Time is often wasted on things of no value. You have that so many times. Some need to experience just what everyone is so different in their thoughts and stages of development so actions come accordingly. See situations as we see them, All are a part of learning and growing. You work on your own a lot because of your speciality of higher and deeper connection to us and give yourself a little time out. Today is a very special day of giving, loving and exchanging. It was all pre planned by us so that now you can enjoy life a little more. We do know how everything is and all is sooner a little clearer and better for all concerned. Too many are after your energy so we have given you extra and more protection. All have to learn how to their own work and stop leaning on others. Tell them to go to us and everyone will benefit, relax and rejoice.

Love and light from us all. TttA

KEEP ALL THINGS IN PROPORTION!

Well now you do needed to be reminded about just that. The balance in between is not enough and too much is to be considered this year. It's extra important to keep in mind that it's different for different people. It's all individual so look at the situation closely before making any changes. Many will only overdo it all at this time as of old traditions. Watch out and see why and look at the preprograming and what is done for you and how easy it would be to carry on. Revalue your actions and only go by your prompting of spirit. You only have to sit quiet for a while and then you can hear what we advise you to do. To sit in silence will also benefit your whole body. The old year according to your calendar will go out and you can look forward to a new start. It's been a learning and in many ways different from all past years. As you evolve you will see and understand more and more. Remember the responsibilities and to pass on knowledge where It's needed. Most you know by now what we mean. More and more spending time with your teachers takes commitment and you have it.

Cheers and joy from. TttA

GOOD ENDING FOR THE OLD YEAR!

Good ending for the old year! We know how much the old year has cost you and how much has been achieved. Many have not understood what the cost is most times necessary not an unusual amount of spirit with emotional and physical. For each one accordingly to their pathway you can never compere or do the same as your fellow man because it's all individual. One thing that you can do is observe and study the pattern of life. Many think that their pattern is of value for their path so they ignore it all. It's always a free will but study life and actions to see what causing what this time of the year. Is always what most people want and think. Many greetings and signs of joy and peace have to remind you about us and come to your door. We send them through people and some angels and stars with sisters and brothers in the universe. A greeting from and long forgotten friends also from many that passed over has come and more will to connect with you and give you peace, health and harmony with joy, so you can be ready for next workload one month from now.

Blessings and joy. TttA

REJOICE!

Be still and just know that all is well. Let's stay close and be together this holiday season. We do know how things are. Enjoy the gifts thoughts and general positive input from so many you have heard and seen from this last year. Many have come to better understand us and where you fit in. Much work is to be done next year and that's why you are resting now and taking stock. Relax and send out love and light to the world and the same who sending you in return. Many have been standing back and not have any idea what to do, they will enter your area next year to let you know. All in good time. Eternal timing is so different so look at it as we do. Let the season give you all cheer, wisdom love and support in full measure. Like we have said so many times, the sun is always there, only covered up many times. It will clear and the light will come down in bigger measure than before. Keep things in perspective and proportion.

Blessings for the Earth and all his inhabitants. TttA

LOVE AND LIGHT FROM ALL OF US!

We wish to all mankind. We are looking at all the kindness,

joy and good actions. It's all a spirit communication. The physical is taken second place this year. First of all remember to put spirit first than all other things will fit into place. We know that you know so tell others. Pass on all the spirited thoughts and knowledge from us. That is what the world needs just now. The lack of eternal joy will only bring sadness and ill health. Let the love and light come forth and warm up so many empty hearts and minds. Light a light and burn incense to cheer you up and your lives. Give thanks to us and your friends for gifts and love. This year's exchange will show up who is who. Don't count the money only the motive behind it all. Look at the hearts of the person and give thanks for all light that have entered in to light up the love. Eternal blessings and health, wisdom love and light.

Keep on working on your growth. TttA

PREPARE FOR THE TIME TO COME!

Most preparations are a sign of planning. Study the pattern and follow through. You all have your special part to do, so do just that. Your kind of work is coming soon get organized and regain your strength to full power. You will be involved in bigger situations, to do your part. Strong leaders are only for a few in between. Listen in very carefully and take notes. Your life is a part from the world for the good of many. Some wonder what you do, they are curious, nosy or plain opportunists. Because of no strong invitation has been given to their confusion has set in. Stay clear of all queries and quandaries. Spend time apart with us and retreat when needed. People that need your love and support will ask if just turning up its assign of panic. Make clear to all that respect is in action. Let us guide you and feed you withy daily wisdom. We are standing by and showing a light on your path. Tests and trials are still around, but not as strong as before. We have tested you severely and all is well.

Love and wisdom. TttA

GIVE THANKS FOR THE YEAR THAT HAS GONE!

Always remember to give thanks for good and not so good events. It's all there for a purpose even if you don't see it at first. The full story will not be told before your life's years have ended. Until the last days of everyone's life you will have an opportunity to look, listen and labour. All in all it's a big lesson for each life to understand and learn more. To be able to grasp the truth takes a lot of time and open mindedness and faith. It might be easy for some and longer time for others. That's not of any value as only the end result counts. We also will give you a reminder about balance. Each person has a special journey each life time to add and understand or complete one lesson. Whatever or which path you have chosen stand back and observe, many will show themselves for what they really are. Never compare or be envious that will not help anyone. It's there because you needed to see what's going on. Practical examples are a good way to learn. Next year you will do more of that and give others guidance-when they are ready to listen.

Blessings and love. TttA

WAIT IN MY PEACE!

Waiting is all you can do now, as much work has been accomplished and many new visions are unfolding. Some very old queries are being answered and sorted out. At first not seeing you will get an easier picture to help you to really see why and how. Don't delay when we say GO! For today and next 4 days stand by and listen in very carefully. We have put you in your castle with the drawbridge up for a purpose. With drawl time to be able to hear and don't waste any time by giving good advice to deaf ears. All energy is given to you to use for yourself and work being done throughout the night. You are regaining much of the old wisdom and will use it in next year's chapter. It will show you more how the connection works and how much can be done in the name of the creator. As we say do only your part and leave us to do ours. Your father is getting to understand and know who you really are. Many questions will be answered and sorted out.

All our love and support TttA

BE STILL!

Silently I speak to the listening ears and hearts. First it's up to you to be still. Do your breathing exercises and then wait. Softly the foot falls are coming towards you and so much love and light. The prince of peace is here once again you know how important it is to wait to learn patient and to be still. You are doing your very best to keep the work up Its a long and winding road at times and at times you can only see a very short distance and then go by faith. The guiding light is there its only not so crowded so our light beams get lost in the midst. When you feel and hear our calling to do something check and listen in and then act with support from us. Wonders are unfolding and so are you. Hold on to that promise and give thanks to all given every day. Nature is a very strong healer and activator, so be outside as much as possible when weather permits. Stay flexible and balanced. We are right on target and all is well. Don't blame us for disasters that humans have not followed through using our advice so the consequences are now showing.

Love and light TttA

CLEAR VIEW!

You will only see the other pattern and your spiritual eye will focus on the glory and beauty. If you can't see, wipe away your thoughts and empty out or any kind of hindrance, remove it at once. If too deep and complex leave it to us to sort out. This time of the year you are thinking of what's gone and what needs to grow and understand. Keep your flame burning and positive thoughts interacting with us and whoever comes to you. So much grief and sadness will be changed to joy and gladness. Be willing to listen and see and move with us and leave yesterday behind. You have experience a lot of healing in all areas. You also got a confirmation about the speed when it happen. We do know how hard it was for you so soon you can tell others that you know.

Blessings and love TttA